A Reader's Guide to West Indian and Black British Literature

David Dabydeen and
Nana Wilson-Tagoe

D1322380

A Hansib/Rutherford Publication

Published by Hansib Publishing in conjunction with the University of Warwick Centre for Caribbean Studies and Department of Continuing Education at Rutherford Press

Hansib Publishing Limited: Tower House, 139/149 Fonthill Road, London N4 3HF, England

Rutherford Press:
UK: 21, Craven Road, Kingston-Upon-Thames, Surrey
Australia: G.P.O. Box 1209, Sydney, NSW 2001
Denmark: Pinds Hus, Geding Søvej 21, 8381 Mundelstrup

Cover Design: Chris Hill
Typesetting: Rutherford Press
Production: Hansib Publishing Limited

Printed in England by: Hansib Printing Limited, Unit 19, Caxton Hill, Hertford, Hertfordshire SG13 7NE, England

Rutherford Press: ISBN 87 88213 21 8
Hansib: ISBN 1 870518 35 7

Hansib Publishing is the longest established and largest black publishing house in Britain, specialising in Black and Third World Literature.

Rutherford Press is an imprint of Dangaroo Press and publishes Black British Literature.

As this is a joint publication and the typesetting was done by Rutherford Press, please note that the spelling of the word "West Indian" is contrary to Hansib's normal house style which uses "Westindian" as one word. This style was introduced in 1973 when the Caribbean Common Market was formed, as a gesture to Caribbean unity. Today it is widely used in the United Kingdom and the Caribbean by many readers of our publications.

To the grandparents, Amy Dabydeen (d. 1985) and Frederick Dabydeen; and to the children, Efau and Kweku Wilson-Tagoe.

Contents

Section 3: Black British Literature

Select Bibliography

Index of Authors

Foreword

This book has the simple aim of introducing new readers to West Indian and Black British Literature. It outlines the history and development of the literatures, highlights their major themes, and suggests texts which best illustrate these themes for further reading. We are particularly interested in promoting the appreciation of these literatures in secondary schools, thereby reaching a large readership of young minds who are the future's writers, scholars, workers and next-door neighbours. Our immediate society and wider world are irrevocably multi-racial: the appreciation of literature can be a crucial activity in deepening people's understanding of each other, of combating ignorance and the violent injustices that spring from ignorance.

The art of labelling is fraught with difficulties and dangers. What *is* 'West Indian' literature? For our purposes, 'West Indian' literature is that written by people from the West Indies (a geographical entity) on subjects relevant to West Indian history and cultures. This may sound a reasonable, even obvious definition, but it is an inadequate label. There have been writers born in the West Indies who emigrated very early in life, and whose creative work deals minimally with West Indian concerns. Equally there have been writers born in Europe and America who have written major books on the West Indies. And what is a 'West Indian' concern that is not a human global concern? Wilson Harris, the Guyanese-born writer, is deeply concerned with the shapes and spaces of the subconscious, a concern provoked by his personal experience of the profoundly strange interior of Guyana. Is his concern 'West Indian', or 'universal' or both?

Black British is even more problematic. For our purposes, 'Black British' literature refers to that created and published in Britain, largely for a British audience, by black writers either born in Britain or who have spent a major portion of their lives in Britain. (We have limited our study to writers of West Indian parentage, since consideration of writers of Asian origin would demand a greatly expanded book). Again this classification sounds reasonable. But what of the term 'black'? Does black denote colour of skin or quality of mind? If the former, what does skin colour have to do with the act of literary creation? If the latter, what is 'black' about black? And what are the literary forms peculiar to 'black' expression, what are the aesthetic structures that differentiate that expression from 'white' expression? In any case what is 'British'? 'British' has to be defined before it can be qualified by the adjective 'black'. Finally, if there are philosophical patterns that can be defined as 'black', and if there are peculiar formal literary constructs based on those patterns, are they sufficient to justify lumping writers together within the boundaries of a singular definition? Where does one 'fit in' age, or class, or gender difference, for example?

These are the kinds of questions which teachers and pupils are encouraged to engage with in approaching or arriving at an understanding of what we have called 'West Indian' and 'Black British' literatures. We use these terms as working definitions and not with the stamp of finality. Our book recommends literary texts which can be fruitfully and pleasurably read for a resolution of these questions.

We are grateful to the Third World Foundation for commissioning parts of the research; to the Commission for Racial Equality for a grant to finance a Teachers' Conference, held at the University of Warwick in 1985, on West Indian literatures; to the Department of Continuing Education (especially Professor Chris Duke, Dr. Tom Schuller and Dr. John Field) at the University of Warwick for its financial support during the 1985/6 academic year; to Janet Bailey and Margaret Barwick (Secretary of Graduate Studies and Librarian's Secretary at the University of Warwick) for typing the manuscript with such patience and efficiency; finally to our undergraduate students at the University (upon whom much of the material in this book was tested) for their enthusiasm and imaginative response to literatures that were initially unfamiliar.

Dr. David Dabydeen
Dr. Nana Wilson-Tagoe
Centre for Caribbean Studies,
University of Warwick, 1986.

Part I: West Indian Literature

Section I: Introduction

In spite of the separations created by geographic distances and the existence of independent West Indian states it is still possible to talk in general terms of a West Indian literature of English expression. The common experience of colonisation, displacement, slavery, indenture, emancipation and nationalism has shaped most West Indian environments, creating a unity of experience that can be identified as particularly West Indian. West Indian literature is in the main, a product of this experience. Its beginnings in the eighteenth and nineteenth centuries, its explosions in the 1930s and 50s and its growth into new dimensions in the late twentieth century reflect the progress of a West Indian engagement with history, with political and social adjustments and with problems of definition, identity and aesthetics.

Such an engagement has evolved through more than a century of West Indian literary activity in poetry, prose, fiction and drama. The movement from the derivative and imitative poetry of the eighteenth and nineteenth centuries, from the often unconscious rejection of the West Indian experience in the early prose fiction towards the social awareness and cultural consciousness of the mid-twentieth century is an indication of a literary trend steeped in the historical development of the West Indies itself. For in the early stages of the region's literature the people in the forefront of literary activity were the white creoles, a minority group with the training and economic power to create

13

a 'creole' literary tradition but often weakened by their cultural allegiance to the metropolis and by an ambivalence towards the islands. The paucity of their literary output and the narrowness of its perspective can be traced for instance, in the deteriorating vision of a fine writer like De Lisser who moved from the social vision of a novel like *Jane's Career* towards exotic romances like *The White Witch of Rosehall.*

The poetry of the period fared even worse in social awareness and in responsibility towards a tradition, and the problem was not just the problem of an imitative and derivative poetry drawing its inspiration and forms from a metropolitan tradition; it was one of an absence of vision and direction. Poets like James Grainger (1723-1765)[1] and M.J. Chapman (1833)[2] wrote without much of a West Indian context, perspective or tradition. Only the black poet Francis Williams,[3] moved perhaps by his own inner tensions, seemed to have seen poetry as a means of voicing personal conflicts and social dilemmas. The emergence of a politically aware and socially conscious literary tradition, it seemed, had to await the improvements in West Indian popular education and the rise of nationalism. Accordingly the years between 1937, when widespread rioting and strikes broke out on the islands leading to labour unrests and demands for self determination, and 1962, when the West Indian federation broke up, constitute the most active and vigorous in the literary history of the islands. They were years of activity and debate marking the rise of political consciousness in the West Indies and the popular anti-colonial agitation which heralded demands for social and political change. The emergence of the 'Beacon Group',[4] a political, radical and creative set active in the labour movement and identified with the independence struggle, gave a new perspective and urgency to literary activity in the West Indies. For these activists were also novelists, poets, short story writers and historians who saw their writing as part of the anti-colonial struggle and of the new sensitivity to economic and social relations. Alfred Mendes's *Pitch Lake* (1934) and *Black Fauns* (1935), and C.L.R. James's *Minty Alley* (1936) widened West Indian perspective by raising questions about the colonial society and giving new depths to the social realism which had informed earlier novels like De Lisser's *Jane's Career. Pitch Lake* for instance, flayed the hollow, spiritually impoverished world of the middle class Portuguese in Trinidad, and *Minty Alley* confronted its educated hero with the lowly, pinched world of the yard.

In poetry the increased self-consciousness and social awareness were reflected in new dimensions especially in the poetry of Una Marson[5] and A.J. Seymour [6] where for the first time, the clichés of the pastoral tradition were giving way to personal exploration and political statement. This vigorous literary activity took place in the atmosphere of a new critical interest in canons and standards. The nature and character of the emerging literature were being debated and defined in the new literary journals of the time, and the ongoing interest in the creole language, in the traditions of the folk and in West Indian historiography,[7] was helping to widen the scope of the debate.

It was from this political and literary context that V.S. Reid's *New Day* (1949) emerged, and it is not surprising that it should have recreated the historical past in order to present a continuity in West Indian experience. This historical perspective was part of the mood of the times, part of the growing sense of a separate West Indian entity and experience. The sense of separateness was not really new in West Indian thought. Jamaican settlers and planters had persistently asserted the distinctiveness of their society and its institutions way back in the eighteenth century. They had often jealously guarded the autonomy and integrity of their Legislative Assembly and even conceived of an internal autonomous Jamaica within the wider framework of Empire. But this sense of 'identity' was frequently obscured by ambiguities and dichotomies. Often, their natural wish for autonomy conflicted with their contempt for the vulgarities of a slave and colonial society. The impact of colonisation complicated the situation by generating a divisive loyalty to the metropolitan culture, and slavery further inhibited their attitudes to the whole idea of freedom, creating a neurotic fear of an enfranchised slave population, and ultimately stifling their aspirations for national independence. Freedom for 'settlers' could not include freedom for slaves. For the slave was not seen then as a force in history, being neither a maker nor a creator of history. Reid's perspective was thus both the continuation of a trend and a widening of its implications. For the first time an imaginative writer had placed the West Indian black in the context of West Indian 'history'. He had rescued him/her from anonymity and made his/her experience and inner reality part of the West Indian aspiration for natural freedom. The West Indian scholar, J.J. Thomas, had admittedly argued the validity of 'negro' history in the West Indies long before, in *Froudacity* (1889), and Mittelholzer had dramatised in almost epic proportions the evolution of Guianese colonial and slave society in the Kaywana triology.[8] But Reid's novel was a development on these, especially in the way it created a particular West Indian sensibility shaped by the peasant environment and way of life of the emancipated slave. But in a sense, Reid's novel was also ironically a reflection of the ambivalence of the nationalist thinking of the time, of its self-consciousness and self-assertion on one hand and of its dependence on the other upon the guidance and goodwill of the metropolis.

The literature of the 50s and 60s was a more rigorous examination of the colonial experience, combining an anti-colonial perspective with a search for new definitions and values. In Guyana, Martin Carter's *Poems of Resistance* (1954) established a strident anti-colonial voice as part of political statement and protest while his later poetry[9] examined the nature of colonial society and the colonial psyche. This was the general direction towards which the literature was moving. The past was again being recreated but in fictional, more imaginative terms that gave writers the leeway to explore the complex consequences of the region's history. For the creative writer of this period the apprehension of history was particularly problematic since the past as manifested in the present seemed both negative and uncreative. West Indian history conceived in terms of progress and development seemed short, uncreative, fragmentary and dependent on values implicit in the language and culture of a colonising power. The imaginative writer's engagement with such a past demanded new and radical approaches to history and for a writer like Lamming, 'history' came to signify more than the history books' definition; it came to mean not a succession of episodes with causal connections but something more active: 'the creation of a situation offering antagonistic opposition and a challenge of survival that had to be met by all involved.[10] The past in other words, was to be confronted and explored, but only with an eye on the future, and for Lamming the future was the future of the Community of people: their self-knowledge, their identity and the re-integration of their personalities. The imaginative medium, not conventional history or anthropology, could grapple with such an exploration and Lamming's novels became ways of investigating and projecting the inner experience of West Indian people, ways of charting the West Indian memory as far as it could go. From *In the Castle of My Skin* through *The Emigrants, Of Age and Innocence, Season of Adventure, Water With Berries,* to *The Pleasures of Exile,* Lamming explored colonial relations and probed the nature of colonial dependence and rebellion. In somewhat similar terms other novelists revealed the reality of West Indian man in ways that no conventional history could have managed. V.S. Reid, who had earlier charted the progress of West Indian experience and sensibility by exploring real history, now examined the emotional and spiritual tensions of colonial relations through a less restricting and inhibiting medium in *The Leopard.* In Jamaica John Hearne reacted in a similar way to the consequences of history, exposing the precariousness and vulnerability of middle class values in novels like *Strangers at The Gate, The Faces of Love* and *Voices Under the Window,* while in Trinidad, V.S. Naipaul and Samuel Selvon assessed the costs and gains of the 'creolisation' of the East Indian in *A House for Mr Biswas* and *A Brighter Sun* respectively. In both novels explorations centred on the creolisation of the East Indian and on the nature and quality of his adjustment in the colonial society. Indian characters moved from enclosed peasant worlds into the wider colonial world, and the movement was in both novels an exploration and a growth in awareness and sensibility, though for Naipaul more than for Selvon possibilities for wholeness, fulfilment and achievement were lessened by the very circumstances of the colonial experience.

The concern with transition and social evolution was not just a concern with progress and growth; it was also an attempt to capture the very meaning and significance of a West Indian world, and this was part of the inspiration behind the proliferation of novels of childhood during this time. Lamming's *In the Castle of My Skin,* Michael Anthony's *The Year in San Fernando,* Drayton's *Christopher,* Ian Mcdonald's *The Humming Bird Tree,* Merle Hodge's *Crick Crack Monkey* and Jean Rhys's *Wide Sargasso Sea* were all in part attempts at capturing and savouring something of the essence of West Indian life through the developing consciousness of the child. Somehow the discovery and identification with this world seemed better and more truthfully revealed through the impressions of the growing child.

In the 60s a similar pre-occupation with meaning and significance underlay Wilson Harris's intense explorations of the impact of history on the West Indian personality. His novels, especially *The Guiana Quartet,*[11] recreated the various aberrations of history in the consciousness of both the oppressor and his victim, enacting not just the linear drama of conquest and defeat but also the dualities and paradoxes of the confrontation, as well as the possibilities for rebirth, reconciliation and a new community.

During this vigorous period of West Indian literary activity, the social world even in its negative manifestation in the slum was an object of exploration. Roger Mais's *The Hills Were Joyful Together* (1953) and *Brother Man* (1954) limited themselves to the conditions of the slum, evoking its deprivations, poverty, frustration and waste as evidence of rural dispossession and urbanisation. These worlds were not the changing and developing worlds of Naipaul, Selvon and Lamming; they were the static enclaves of the urban castaways, those whom industrialisation had flushed out and abandoned. Mais sought to highlight the social neglect of the slums while at the same time revealing the indomitable will of the people and the healing unifying power of the communal spirit. In the early 60s Orlando Patterson was to evoke the same background in the *Children of Sisyphus* (1964), demonstrating the same social concern but revealing frustration and escapism as the ultimate absurdity of the West Indian condition.

The concern with the consequences of history, with the social world and its impact on West Indian sensibility, led almost naturally to another major theme in the 50s and 60s: the theme of

Harper Collins Crime Night

Claire Seeber launches *Lullaby*

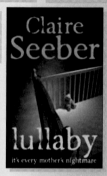

Editor, Keshini Naidoo, on crime writing and the new Avon inprint

7.45 for 8–9.30pm
Tuesday 26 February 2008
Free admission

Lewisham Library
199/201 Lewisham High Street
Lewisham SE13 6LG
tel. 020 8314 9800
www.lewisham.gov.uk/libraries

Reader's Guide to
West Indian+ Black
British Literature

Ref ~~810.9~~ 818

History of literature
in the Caribbean
809.89729

emigration. The concern was a response both to a historical phenomenon and a psychological colonial problem. In the 50s and 60s West Indians were actually emigrating from the islands to the metropolis, in search of what they called a 'better break', though in some sense they were also manifesting a colonial syndrome, a belief in a shared heritage with the mother country and the Western world. Novel after novel, poem after poem explored the pleasures and perils of exile and their effects on the sensibilities of West Indians. Lamming's *The Emigrants, Water With Berries* and *The Pleasures of Exile;* Selvon's *Ways of Sunlight, The Lonely Londoners, Moses Migrating, Moses Ascending;* Brathwaite's *Rights of Passage* and recently the novels of Austin Clarke[12] have all revealed the enlarged consciousness of the emigrant side by side with his peculiar disorientation in an alien world. Increasingly however, the idea of migration has become almost a global phenomenon and a new extension of West Indian consciousness and vision has already begun to emerge in England and North America.

This exciting progress of theme, vision and form in the West Indian novel has not always been matched in the region's poetry. In the 1940s and 50s West Indian poets and dramatists clearly lagged behind the novelists. Still groping for distinctive voices they had not acquired the depth of theme and authority of vision that the novelists had achieved. Claude McKay's[13] experiments with dialect and folk forms in the 1920s and his articulation of the divided Afro-Caribbean consciousness in poems like 'Outcast' had offered significant directions, but it was not until the 60s with the poetry of Louise Bennett, Eric Roach, Derek Walcott and Edward Brathwaite that these forms and themes began to be handled with maturity and complexity. The Calypsonian Sparrow[14] and the poet Louise Bennett[15] explored various dimensions of the tradition of folk poetry, exploring the orality of the form and enhancing the performance quality of poetry and song. In the written medium Walcott was grappling with themes of displacement and spiritual impoverishment in *The Castaway* and looking for ways in which the artist could transcend these in his effort to be creative. For all his cynicism and despair however, he did manage to retain a sense of the possibilities of the poetic experience and to progress through

The Gulf and *Another Life* towards a view of the artist as capable of freeing his people by returning them unto themselves through the very act of naming them, of capturing their lives, their landscape and their language. Accordingly his experiments in the Trinidad workshop with dialect, folk forms and folk mythologies in plays like *The Sea at Dauphin, T-Jean and His Brothers* and *Dream on Monkey Mountain* helped to establish a most vibrant tradition in West Indian drama, realising his hopes of making 'heraldic men' out of 'foresters and fishermen'.[16]

Brathwaite, the other major poet of the 60s, responded to the apparent void in the region by exploring the creolising process itself and seeing in the adjustments and adaptations to slavery and colonisation, creative possibilities that could provide a context of history and a source for a tradition of poetry. His trilogy: *Rights of Passage, Masks* and *Islands* recreated and appraised the New World experience, revealing its manifestations in the variety of Caribbean musical structures and in the very language of the creolised folk with its distinctive core of perception and sensibility. These explorations of the 60s, the personal dialogues, the experiments with song, dialect, sermon and ritual, established a tradition of orality in written poetry, creating an authority to which poets of the 70s and 80s could refer in their search for forms based on indigenous models. Thus, far from striving to establish a tradition, relying for instance, on external (often) metropolitan models, West Indian poets of the 70s wrote with a sense of an already existing tradition. Wayne Brown's *On The Coast* though principally an appraisal of the new national order, took on some of the perceptual models of the older Walcott in the 'Castaway' poems, and several of the younger poets of the 70s saw in Brathwaite's oral models a fresh and exhilarating medium.

In general the poetry of the early 70s wavered between an appreciation of the revolutionary and radical imagination ushered in by the Black Power movement, and an awareness of its level of rhetoric and self-delusion. The spirit and sensibility of the age were often captured in the ambivalences in the works of poets like Roger McTair, Victor Questel, Wayne Browne, Anthony McNeill and Dennis Scott. Their poetry relates to the poetry of the younger generation in the way in which the West

Indian experience continues to be recreated and appraised in the 80s.

In the contemporary 80s the metropolitan experience has for historical reasons become a notable influence on West Indian poetry and literature. British West Indians have either provided dimensions of their experiences or re-appraised the colonial experience with imaginations nurtured by wider perceptions of colonial relations. But the greatest influence on contemporary West Indian poetry has been without doubt, the complementary relationships of the oral and written traditions. It is really the recognition and exploitation of the ordinary speaking voice as an expression of feeling and perception that has given West Indian poetry a distinctiveness and authority capable of preserving the uniqueness of the West Indian experience.

Notes

1. James Grainger, *Sugar Cane* (London, 1764).
2. M.J.Chapman, *Barbados* (London, 1833).
3. Francis Williams, 'Ode to George Haldane' in Edward Long, *History of Jamaica* (London, 1774).
4. These were mostly literary people and political activists associated with the Jamaican monthly publication, *The Beacon*: Albert Gomes, Alfred Mendes and C.L.R. James. The literary output of *The Beacon* was complemented by other publications: *Focus* edited by Edna Manley, *Kyk-ove-al* (1945/61) edited in Guyana by A.J. Seymour and *BIM* edited in Barbados by Frank A. Collymore.
5. Una Marson, *Tropic Reveries* (Kingston, Jamaica, 1930).
6. A.J. Seymour, *Verse* (Georgetown, Guyana, 1937).
7. See, (a) J.J. Thomas, *The Theory and Practice of Creole Grammar*, (Port-of-Spain, 1869).
     (b) Martha Beckwith, *Jamaica Anansi Stories* (New York, 1924).
         Jamaica Proverbs (New York, 1925).
     (c) C.L.R. James, *The Black Jacobins* (New York, 1938).
     (d) Eric Williams, *Capitalism and Slavery* (Chapel Hill, 1944).
         The Negro in the Caribbean (Washington, 1942).
         Education in the British West Indies (Port-of-Spain, 1950).
     (e) Elsa Goveia, *A Study on the Historiography of the British West Indies* (Mexico, 1956).

8. See, Edgar Mittelholzer, *Children of Kaywana* (London, 1952).
    The Harrowing of Hubertus (London, 1954).
    Kaywana Blood (London, 1958).

9. See, Martin Carter, *Poems of Succession* (London, 1977); *Poems of Affinity* (Georgetown, Guyana Release Publishers, 1980).

10. George Lamming, *The Pleasures of Exile* (London, 1960).

11. See, Wilson Harris (a) *Palace of the Peacock* (1960); (b) *The Far Journey of Oudin* (1962); *The Whole Armour* (1962); *The Secret Ladder* (1963). All published by Faber and Faber, London.

12. See, Austin Clarke, *The Meeting Point* (London, 1967); *The Bigger Light* (Boston & Toronto, 1975).

13. Claude McKay, *Songs of Jamaica* (Kingston, Jamaica, 1912); *Constab Ballads* (London 1912); *Selected Poems,* (New York, 1953).

14. The Mighty Sparrow (Slinger Francisco), acknowledged champion of calypso.

15. Louise Bennett, *Dialect Verse* (Kingston, Jamaica, 1942); *Jamaica Labrish* (Kingston, Jamaica, 1966).

16. First known as the Basement Theatre Workshop, it was founded by Derek Walcott in 1959.

Section 2: Selected Themes

A. Anti-imperialism and Nationalism

In West Indian literature the themes of anti-imperialism and nationalism were part of the political movement for independence and part of the cultural nationalism which was its manifestation. The consciousness of a West Indian people with a character, history and aspirations separate from the metropolis was an underlining ideology in the nationalist movement and was reflected in several dimensions in the literature of the mid-twentieth century. There was on one hand, the straightforward anti-colonial literature, mostly poetry, in which writers were single-mindedly committed to the socio-political function of poetry and in which the poem was less an imaginative evocation than a strident protest expressing outrage at colonial repression. This tradition of anti-colonial protest poetry, begun by McKay, continued by George Campbell and exploited to the full by Martin Carter in *Poems of Resistance,* was the most straight-forward form of anti-imperialist literature in the early stages. On several other literary levels feelings of anti-imperialism and notions of nationalism were expressed in less direct and more subtle explorations. In the novel a new interest in history, in the historical process and in the continuity of historical experience, marked a new West Indian awareness, which was a challenge to nine-teenth century assumptions about the historylessness of the region. V.S. Reid's *New Day,* Samuel Selvon's *A Brighter Sun* and Roger Mais's *The Hills were Joyful Together* were all attempts at creating this distinctive experience and character.

Towards the late 50s and in the early 60s however, anti-imperialist themes acquired greater variation and depth. Novelists and poets set themselves the more rigorous task of analysing the colonial society, of assessing the colonial's rebellion and exploring his psyche. Although these themes were not straightforward nationalistic themes, pitting coloniser against colonised as in some of the earlier protest poetry, their nationalist affirmations centred on the ways in which they sought to clarify and define the West Indian experience. Each novelist seems to have attempted to understand his relationship to the colonial experience and to have sought a vision from his exploration and analysis. Lamming's concern with the nature of true freedom in *Of Age and Innocence* and *Season of Adventure* was in part an attempt to come to terms with a colonial status and to transcend the conditions it imposed. For him, true freedom was dependent on the quality of protest and rebellion which were in turn related to the people's sense of history and their link with the rural organic world of the peasant. For Naipaul, true freedom, the link with landscape and the sense of community as envisaged by Lamming, seemed an impossibility. The very wrongness of the colonial adventure, the irrevocable disability it engendered, he felt, created barriers between the colonial and true freedom. In both *A House for Mr Biswas* and *The Mimic Men* his characters struggled against these barriers, achieving either limited and fragile personal niches in the general chaos or a more cathartic and personal understanding of their situation.

The concern with the colonial experience and the colonial psyche led invariably to other variations in the anti-colonial theme: the Prospero-Caliban relationship. It was an interesting and revolutionary variation especially in the way it challenged the usual historical assumptions about the colonised as an object rather than a subject of history. A great deal of Walcott's concern in *The Castaway* was, for instance, directed towards subverting and challenging these very assumptions. His skilful manipulation of symbolism and language especially in the 'Crusoe' poems offered dimensions of colonial relations that challenged the dominant myth of Crusoe as the heroic European settler struggling against odds to maintain supremacy and provide light and guidance in a colonial society. His explorations transcended the usual images of master/slave/servant and highlighted ways in which the colonial sometimes manipulated the relationship to his advantage and achieved an often unique personal development in the process. In these poems the colonised became not just the converted cannibal moulded to the coloniser's faith; he became the very human 'Friday' whose personal and separate development perceived contradictions and failures in the new faith itself. This rounded view of Friday as human, self-aware and perceptive, not only endowed him with a subjectivity and an identity but also revealed a level of subtlety in his relationship with Crusoe.

Lamming undertook similar explorations in *The Pleasures of Exile, Water With Berries* and *Natives of My Person*, projecting the colonial 'Caliban' as possessing a unique insight into the coloniser's consciousness and motivation. His reading of Shakespeare's *The Tempest* in *The Pleasures of Exile* was in a major sense a metaphorical view of West Indian colonisation and of the psychology of colonial relations. It was also in the final analysis, an attempt to create a future from the past, a way of pushing colonial relations beyond that legacy of domination and subordination which 'history' ordinarily imposes. For Lamming this future involved a transformation of past relations and this was possible only when the past, endowed with different meanings, generated new soils for new beginnings: 'The mystery of the colonial is this: where he remains alive, his instinct, always and forever creative, must choose a way to change the meaning and perspective of this ancient tyranny.'

The entire range of Lamming's work as a novelist springs from this perspective and his novels concern themselves with analysis and explorations on both personal and public levels. The drama is always a struggle to escape the cage of personal (and public) history, a struggle to choose a way of changing the meaning and perspective of the 'ancient tyranny'. In *Water With Berries,* Lamming's most complex and intense drama of colonial relations, the colonial does finally survive and is able to choose and act. Like a crab among rocks Lamming's Teeton emerges slowly from the furnace of the coloniser's (the Dowager's) grave to answer the political call of 'the Gathering', representing his messianic future. The experience is altogether a spiritual and hugely symbolic one, and the catharsis merges into an apocalyptic vision of revolution and promise. In most of Lamming's anti-colonial novels the burden of re-orientation and change is normally the burden of the colonised. But choice and change involve a future which also includes a dialogue and an understanding with the coloniser, and the changed relationship between coloniser and colonised, between Prospero and Caliban, becomes Lamming's major emphasis in *Natives of My Person*. The personal drama is principally the coloniser's drama and is necessitated by Caliban's assertion of freedom, by his new vision of himself as a 'possibility of spirit which might fertilise and extend the resources of any human vision'. To accept this vision of Caliban in a new relationship, Prospero has to evaluate his own place in a changed world and re-examine those values which once sanctioned his acts as a coloniser. *Natives Of My Person* is the drama of this revaluation and is Lamming's attempt at transcending the 'historybook' story of colonisation.

Interestingly the themes of anti-imperialism and nationalism have continued to engage West Indian writers since the explosion of these very themes in the 50s and 60s. Each generation seems to be engaged by particular dimensions of the fundamental ideas. Wayne Brown's *On The Coast,* a product of the 70s might for instance appear to be treading the old ground of Walcott and Brathwaite in the 60s, but the poet's bitter attack on the continuing colonial syndrome of dependence and self-rejection has an edge of anger and bitterness which gives him a special emphasis. On the other hand Dabydeen's *Slave Song,* published in the 80s, explores the colonial experience through the imaginative reconstruction of the private world of slave and indentured labourer: an inner world of anger, pain, frustration, brutality and fantasy; an imaginative fusion of present and 'past' which as Lamming has argued, neither 'history' nor 'anthropology' could evoke.

These variations of the anti-imperialist and nationalist themes indicate the extent to which, from the very beginning, the act of writing in the West Indies has been part of the new national consciousness and self-awareness. The very proliferation of these themes and the continual re-appraisals reveal the colonial experience as the single most important determinant in the making of the West Indian people.

Major Texts

1. V.S. Reid *New Day* (New York: Knopf, 1949; Republished in Heinemann Caribbean Writers Series).

The novel sees Jamaica's constitutional freedom of 1944 as an inevitable sequel to the Morant Bay rebellion of 1865. Reid uses the Campbells, a fictional family of mixed African and European ancestry as the cultural and political link in this historical progress, and his novel charts the movement from a fiery but ineffectual radicalism towards a responsible political leadership in which a combined force of workers and the educated class achieves political realisation through reasoned argument.

2. George Lamming *Of Age and Innocence* (London: Michael Joseph, 1958; London: Alison and Busby, 1981).

Lamming's third novel explores the pitfalls and failures of nationalist aspirations in the West Indies. Carefully plotted to reflect the multi-racial complexity of the West Indies, it dramatises the historical disabilities which West Indians must overcome in order to achieve true unity and freedom.

3. George Lamming *Natives of My Person* (New York: Holt, Rinehart and Winston, 1972).

Lamming describes this novel as a way of going forward by making a complete return to the beginnings. In it, he attempts to understand the colonial experience and colonial relations by examining the very roots of West Indian colonisation, concentrating on the drama of the coloniser's voyage, (from Europe to the slave coast and to the West Indies), his motivation, his psyche and the eventual brutalisation of his personality.

4. Samuel Selvon *Turn Again Tiger* (London: MacGibbon and Kee, 1958; London: Longman, 1962).

Written six years after *A Brighter Sun* and featuring the same creolised Indian peasant, this novel recreates the environment and social context of the colonial plantation, complete with its hierarchy of white supervisor, overseer, time keeper and labourers. The protagonist's confrontation with the situation and its moral and psychological reflections becomes an examination of his own relationship to the colonial experience. The mere process of creolisation, Selvon implies, is finally not the whole answer to the quest for freedom and realisation.

5. V.S. Naipaul *The Mimic Men* (London: André Deutsch, 1967).

Naipaul's novel examines the relationship between the colonial experience and nationalist assertion in the West Indies, showing how freedom itself is limited and impaired by the permanent disabilities of the colonial experience. Its world is a grim one in which the dismantling of the external colonial order leaves only chaos because the fragmented ex-slave society of displaced people has no centre to hold the society together. Nationalism in such a context, Naipaul implies, is ultimately ineffective, appealing only to race and colour and offering only drama and violence.

6. Martin Carter *Poems of Resistance* (London: Lawrence and Wishart, 1954); *Poems of Succession* (London: New Beacon Books, 1977).

Carter's poems, written in the ferment of political resistance to colonialism, are perhaps the most vocal and tormented anti-imperialist assertions of the period. Composed almost as dialogues between the poet and the conditions of his existence, between the poet and the Caribbean man, and between the poet and the coloniser, they argue the historical necessity for revolution and transformation, projecting a vision of freedom and liberation in a future that is also (ironically) apprehended as vulnerable.

7. Derek Walcott *The Castaway And Other Poems* (London: Jonathan Cape, 1965).

In this collection of poems Walcott's persona, the artist figure, responds to the colonial experience as revealed in the physical and human landscape of the Caribbean. Here, the historical experience of people and landscape is as relevant as the artist's isolation and estrangement, and the poet takes on the burden of making meaning and drawing out significances.

8. Wayne Brown *On The Coast* (London: André Deutsch, 1972).

Brown's collection is essentially an evaluation of the colonial experience almost in the tradition of Walcott's early poetry. The evocations span three phases of the historical experience, manifesting the harshly anti-colonial moods of Walcott's early poetry. In 'Conquistador', 'Red Hill' and 'Drought', he recreates the wasteland of empire, the self-contempt generated by racial inferiority and the persisting colonial psychology.

9. David Dabydeen *Slave Song* (Denmark and U.K.: Dangaroo Press, 1984).

The poems in *Slave Song* bring to life the ordinary humdrum life of slave and Indian colonial peasant, depicting it as shaped both by the rigour and brutality of plantation life and by those rare moments of order, compassion and tenderness which are also ironically, part of his sensibility. Those instances in which his sexual fantasies about the white woman become conscious acts of subversion and liberation manifest a human presence in spite of a colonial self-abasement.

10. Edward Brathwaite *Islands* (London: Oxford University Press, 1969); *The Arrivants: A New World Trilogy* (London: Oxford University Press, 1973).

Brathwaite's poetry in *Islands* challenges the usual colonial view of the Caribbean as an uncreative product of the imperial order. His sensitivity to the creative areas of West Indian experience in the Caribbean and his recognition of a spiritual numinous quality in the peasant's sensibility inspire his hopes of redemption and restoration. The poems reflect this, alternating between visions of sterility in which all memory is lost, and visions of hope in which the poet himself becomes a priest, attempting a recovery of the word.

B. The Treatment of Race

As a fundamental aspect of the colonial experience, race has always been a crucial issue in colonial relations and has surfaced in various dimensions in the literature of the West Indies. The simplicity of the colonial society, Naipaul observes in *The Loss of Eldorado*, was the very simplicity of its values of money and race, and in the colour-structured society, unified only by the consensual acceptance of the inferiority of 'negro-ness', race was an appalling definer of value. It came up not only in relations between European white master and black slave, but also between the various gradations of the colour hierarchy. Such consistent debasement of 'negro-ness' had two major psychological repercussions: it instilled in the black slave an overwhelming awe of everything white and at the same time bred a sense of inferiority and self-abasement in his innermost consciousness. The emancipation of slaves and the exhilaration of freedom which accompanied it did nothing much to change the general thinking on race; rather the importation of indentured labour from India into a number of West Indian islands introduced a new racial element, complicating the white/black dichotomy. White, coloured, African, East Indian affected basically separate racial identities, fearful, suspicious and often contemptuous of each other. The colonial society, reflecting most of these tensions, remained fragmented and unsettled, a prey to racially inspired conflict and violence. In West Indian literature the racial theme has generally been associated with the theme of history, and the best of West Indian writing on the subject has seen its ramifications as a historical legacy and has explored possibilities of transcending its negative effects. As part of the new nationalist self-awareness and re-definition, writers explored the psychology of race and colour in the consciousness of black West Indians almost as an exorcism of a deep-seated racial inferiority. V.S. Reid provided an interesting exploration of the theme in *The Leopard* (1958), an imaginative evocation against the background of the Mau Mau rebellion, of relations between white and black and between mulatto and black; aspects which he had suggested but left unexplored in *New Day*. Like

Reid, Walcott and Lamming explored similar confrontations in *Dream On Monkey Mountain, T-Jean and His Brothers* and *Water With Berries* respectively, and in all these works the underlying idea was the decapitation of the dominant white master image, whether it was manifested in the white goddess as in *Dream,* or in the Devil as in *T-Jean,* or in the benevolent Dowager as in *Water With Berries.* In all three situations the black colonial had to annihilate the dominant racial image in order to be free, for as Walcott has said, getting rid of his overwhelming awe of everything white is the first step every colonial must take.

On another level the racial theme explored the West Indian's confrontation with Africa as a racial and cultural symbol. It was in a sense a confrontation with self, a coming to terms with origin and a purging of fear and shame. The black West Indian had grown to accept the racial and cultural inferiority of Africa, and for him this was a crucial confrontation. In Reid's *The Leopard* it took the form of the tortuous relationship between the 'mulatto' Toto and his black father Nebu; in Lamming's *Season of Adventure* it was dramatised in the relationship between the middle-class Fola and the voodoo ceremony of souls; in *Other Leopards* it formed the entire drama of Lionel Froad's ambivalent response to the African past; in Brathwaite's *Masks* it consisted in a positive evocation of an African world and culture which the poet could not possess but to which he felt related. These levels of confrontation were in a sense acts of purgation that led to the black West Indian's revaluation of himself/herself and his/her place in the world. Other aspects of the theme were explored in a different sense by Wilson Harris in novels like *Palace of The Peacock,* the *Secret Ladder* and *Heartland.* Here the confrontation was not so much between ancestor and a particular racial group as between Amerindian/African ancestor and the entire Caribbean consciousness. For Harris not only believed in the unity of all peoples but also in the possibility of capturing the subtle discontinuities in the region's history as a means of illuminating the Caribbean psyche and extending its sensibility.

Among writers of East Indian descent, the need to exorcise fear and shame, was, for obvious historical reasons, not so urgent a theme. Thus in writers like Naipaul racial themes surfaced mostly as an awareness of the loss of racial and cultural homogeneity or as a recognition of the barriers which ethnicity and the plural society placed on the political and social prospects of West Indian societies. *A House for Mr Biswas* is for instance, in one sense, a redefinition of 'Indianness' in the context of a disordered colonial and multi-racial society while *The Mimic Men* is a drama of the historical and racial barriers against true freedom and nationhood. Naipaul saw these barriers and disabilities as generated by history, by the very wrongness of the artificial societies of the West Indies. For him, these were permanent disabilities over which there could be no transcendence, but for writers like Selvon, Mittelholzer and Lamming who also explored the racial theme, possibilities for transcendence existed in people's understanding, in their capacity to re-order their societies.

Major Texts

1. V.S. Reid *The Leopard* (London: Heinemann, 1958; Republished in Heinemann Caribbean Writers Series; New York: Collier Books, 1971).

Set against the background of the racial conflicts and hatred of Kenya's 'Mau Mau' struggle, the novel explores the consciousness of race and racial identity as part of the process of resistance against white oppression. On another level it is a drama of the tortuous relationship between the 'Mulatto' (Western black) and his African origins. A greater part of the action in the forest concentrates on the 'Mulatto' and the dying African, and the drama is projected as the 'Mulatto's' inward journey towards knowledge, understanding and acceptance of his origins.

2. George Lamming *Season of Adventure* (London: Michael Joseph, 1960).

The novel, which enacts what Lamming has called 'the backward glance', is the drama of his middle-class heroine's dialogue with her forgotten racial self and of the political and social repercussions of this adventure. The tonelle, the ceremony of souls and the forest reserve represent areas of African folk experience which the heroine has always rejected out of fear and shame. Her confrontation with the ceremony begins a process that leads her to self-awareness, understanding and consequently to a major political action on behalf of her society.

3. Edward Brathwaite *Masks* (London: Oxford University Press, 1968; published as part of *The Arrivants* by Oxford University Press, 1973).

Brathwaite's long poem is an enactment of the modern West Indian's return to Africa, an experience which Brathwaite broadens with a simultaneous evocation of the circumstances of the Middle Passage and of Africa's own historical progress and development up to that time. These three areas of experience to which the poet-persona responds through his borrowed masks present a comprehensive African world which the poet cannot possess but to which he feels himself related. This awareness and acknowledgement of kinship not only purge his fear and shame about the past but also lead to an understanding of the sources of his West Indian identity.

4. Denis Williams *Other Leopards* (London: Hutchinson, 1963; Republished in Heinemann Caribbean Writers Series).

Williams's novel charts the difficulties and dilemmas of the West Indian's quest for origins. The novel's central character, Lionel Froad is caught between two visions of himself, the cultivated European image which he possesses and the ancestral image which he thinks he ought to acquire. His divided consciousness is a disability that leaves him feeling empty, insubstantial and doggedly set to find himself in Africa. But identity is not something we merely pick up and wear, and Williams's hero, caught between a genuine desire for a racial identity and an honest alienation from tradition and politics in Africa, ends up defeated and disoriented.

5. Derek Walcott *Dream On Monkey Mountain* (New York: Farrar, Strauss and Giroux, 1977).

Walcott's play identifies the fantasies about whiteness and ancestral connections with Africa as the major fantasies which pre-occupy, confuse and shape the psyche of West Indian man. His central character is caught between the two fantasies. His vision of himself as a descendant of African kings and as a revolutionary saviour of his African tribe is ironically inspired by a white blonde goddess, symbol of that very whiteness which is the antithesis of his ordinary perception of himself as black, ugly and undesirable. Are the fantasies about African origins inspired by fantasies about whiteness? The acting out of such fantasies is a process of understanding and self-knowledge, but the ultimate self-knowledge, Walcott implies, is the ability to liberate oneself eventually, acknowledging only the green beginnings of the West Indies as one's true origin.

6. Wilson Harris *The Secret Ladder* (London: Faber and Faber, 1963).

The novel explores racial identity and the quest for origins as a need to understand and transform Caribbean beginnings. Its action involves a confrontation between the middle-class cultivated surveyor, his racially mixed crew and the community of Africans, descendants of runaway slaves. The confrontation explores what Harris feels should be the Caribbean man's relationship with the ancestor.

7. Edgar Mittelholzer *A Morning At The Office* (London: Hogarth Press, 1950; Republished in Heinemann Caribbean Writers Series).

The action of Mittelholzer's novel about Trinidad is compressed into the precise time scheme of a particular morning but it succeeds in dramatising the workings of a stratified, colour-based, colonial society. The characters reflect the class and racial situations of Trinidad society and their relationships are conditioned by their various historical experiences. The author's delineation points to the need for compassion between people and for the integration of the different peoples and cultures of Trinidad.

8. V.S. Naipaul *The Suffrage of Elvira* (London: André Deutsch, 1958).

The novel is a comic evocation of the racial, religious and cultural mix-up which is the historical legacy of Trinidad society. Although the campaign for the elections demonstrates an easy interaction between racial and religious groups, the novel's action points to the failure of true unity and democracy. Under pressure, Trinidadians cluster into their racial groups. The election for all its underlying comedy proves a serious point about the simplicity of the colonial society and its simple values of race and money.

9. George Lamming *Of Age And Innocence* (London: Michael Joseph, 1958; London: Alison and Busby, 1981).

The racial theme in Lamming's novel resides in the prospects and fortunes of the political alliance between the three racial groups and on the progress of the friendship between the four young boys, representatives of the four racial groups in San Cristobal. The novel balances and contrasts the two sets of relationships, measuring the forces at work in each situation. Among the older politicians the ideals of freedom and unity struggle against the prejudices and attitudes engendered by history, ultimately crumbling in the face of colonial opposition and intrigue. In contrast the young boys appear free from fixed perceptions and notions. Their vision represents a whole new way of seeing, and it is in their strengths that Lamming locates the racial ideal and the future.

10. Samuel Selvon *A Brighter Sun* (London: Allan Wingate, 1952; London: Longman, 1979).

The novel is basically a novel about growth, and part of this growth consists in the East Indian hero's perception of himself as part of a multi-racial creole society. The very idea of a new cosmopolitan town as the location for the action and the complementary presence of an Afro-Trinidadian couple not only suggest Selvon's special pleading but also a movement forward from enclosed racial entities.

C. The Theme of Childhood

The theme of childhood and with it the idea of growth from innocence to maturity has been a recurrent theme in West Indian literature. Its popularity seems to stem from the very notion of development which it entails. The idea of capturing environment and experience from childhood right through to maturity is for the West Indian writer almost like a re-living of a West Indian experience, a savouring of its essential character. In all the novels about childhood the child protagonist is almost always engaged in recording the impact of a particular environment or experience. Michael Anthony's two novels, *The Year In San Fernando* (1965) and *Green Days By The River* are both novels about a child's progress through a particular world. *The Year In San Fernando* records the consciousness of a rural boy as he responds and adjusts to the city and its peculiar ethos. As readers we are drawn into the fresh unbiased responses of the child as he reacts to landscape and people, and as he develops in knowledge, understanding and judgement. Sometimes, as in *Green Days*, we witness in the child's growth the loss of childhood spontaneity and the beginnings of adult choice with its necessary calculation and compromise. Anthony's novels are in the main uncompromisingly committed to the child's experience. The reader is led to view the world as the child experiences it and is thus limited to his uncomplicated perceptions and awarenesses.

In other novels about childhood the child's experiences become part of the novel's social and political vision and are often controlled and shaped by the overall point of view of the writer. In Merle Hodge's *Crick Crack Monkey* the young heroine's experiences are crucial both for her personal development and as an illustration of the novel's theme of cultural confusion and insecurity. Thus while the overall point of view is the heroine's (as in Anthony's novels), Hodge controls and manipulates it to suggest crucial ironies against her, ironies which are part of the novelist's deliberate control of point of view in the interest of a social vision. In Drayton's *Christopher* the situation is made a little easier by the novelist's omniscient point of view. The boy hero, like Jean Rhys's white creole heroine, grows up in the era of the decline of white influence in Barbados, and his personality and perceptions are influenced by class tensions between the white creoles themselves and by racial tensions between whites and blacks on the island. Unlike Rhys's heroine, who is crushed by her feelings of alienation and disconnection the boy Christopher grows up turning inwards, developing his relations with the land, nurturing his artistic sensibilities and also through his warm relations with his nurse developing an understanding of the black world around him.

In Lamming the world of childhood becomes part of the colonial ethos and of the general disintegration evoked and dramatised in *In the Castle of My Skin*. The children's responses to their environment, their interpretations of adult standards and their confusions about history and race reflect both the confusions and fantasies of childhood and the sensibilities of a colonial upbringing. The very tensions between them, the eventual separations that send each child on a separate course, are all part of the social forces that divide colonial society. Although Lamming uses the children's lives to suggest a typical West Indian childhood, his emphasis is eventually on the maturing consciousness of his child narrator and hero. Thus boy 'G' whose personal and political growth are finally charted and linked with the frustrations and the disintegration of the old order becomes Lamming's portrait of the sensitive and alienated artist.

It is not always that the theme of childhood is explored as a progress towards physical and emotional maturity. Sometimes entire areas of a child's perception are opened simply through his perception of people around him. The boy narrator in Naipaul's *Miguel Street* presents such a vision of childhood. His evocation and presentation of the dramas around him reveal both the environment that has shaped him and the way he himself perceives it. In this case maturity is not measured in terms of physical growth but in the increasing quality of perception with which the child narrator presents his stories and his perceptions.

Major Texts

1. Michael Anthony *The Year in San Fernando* (London: André Deutsch, 1965; Republished in Heinemann Caribbean Writers Series).

The novel deals principally with a crucial year of adjustment in the life of a child. A young rural boy is constrained by his family's poor circumstances to move in with a better-off family in the city, and the novel charts his responses, perceptions and personal growth in the course of a year.

2. Michael Anthony *Green Days by the River* (London: André Deutsch, 1967; Republished in Heinemann Caribbean Writers Series).

An evocation of a Trinidad childhood, concentrating on a young boy's response to the landscape and the world around him. It is also the story of a boy's gradual social and sexual awakening.

3. Geoffrey Drayton *Christopher* (London: Collins, 1959).

Drayton's novel depicts the childhood of a young white creole boy, growing up in the West Indies at a time when the economic power of the old planter class had been usurped by the new merchant class of white upstarts. The tensions and resentments between the two classes of white people dramatise themselves in the estrangement between the boy's parents and in the boy's own brooding loneliness throughout the novel. His growth into maturity is however, presented as a complex and interesting process of self-discovery and social awareness.

4. Jean Rhys *Wide Sargasso Sea* (London: Hutchinson, 1966; Republished by Penguin Books, Harmondsworth, 1968).

The novel recreates the changed circumstances and the psychological terror of Jamaican white creoles at finding themselves after emancipation swamped by a free and hostile black population. Rhys's heroine lives under the psychological strain of these times, and the novel dramatises her sense of menace and insecurity as well as the gradual alienation that contribute to the disorientation and madness in her adult life. *Wide Sargasso Sea* is the story of the first Mrs. Rochester, the mad wife in C. Bronte's *Jane Eyre.*

5. Ian McDonald *The Humming Bird Tree* (London: Heinemann, 1969; Republished in Heinemann Caribbean Writers Series).

McDonald evokes with regret and nostalgia the spontaneity and romance of a Trinidad childhood. The romance between his white creole hero and the East Indian girl cuts across the racial and class barriers solidly built by the island's historical legacy. But this illusion of possibility is shown as part of the innocence of childhood itself. In his maturity the hero confronts the reality of his situation as a member of the white oligarchy and is unable to break out of the prison of history.

6. George Lamming *In the Castle of My Skin* (London: Michael Joseph, 1953. Republished by Longman, London, 1979).

Lamming recreates a typical Barbadian childhood as part of the social world he presents in this novel. The group of young boys whose feelings, responses and fantasies occupy several chapters, present a picture of what it was like to be a child growing up in the 1930s.

7. Merle Hodge *Crick Crack Monkey* (London: André Deutsch, 1970; Republished in Heinemann Caribbean Writers Series).

Hodge's heroine grows up amidst the class and cultural confusions in the Trinidad of the mid-twentieth century. Intelligent and sensitive, she nevertheless suffers from insecurity and self-rejection when moved from a raw but humane lower class world into a pretentious and artificial one. Although the novel's ironies show up the confusions of the social world, the heroine's own personal trauma and her dilemmas about race and culture are never really resolved.

8. V.S. Naipaul *Miguel Street* (London: André Deutsch, 1959; Republished by Penguin Books, Harmondsworth, 1971).

The stories in *Miguel Street* present us with a child's view of the world around him, and although not necessarily about his progress towards physical and emotional maturity, these are demonstrated in the quality of perception with which he presents, comments upon and judges the various experiences he evokes.

9. Derek Walcott *Another Life* (London: Jonathan Cape, 1973).

In this autobiographical poem Walcott charts the landmarks in the childhood and growth of a young St. Lucian boy. It is in some sense Walcott's portrait of the artist as a growing child and it recreates the various social, cultural and spiritual influences that shaped his personality and his artistic sensibilities.

10. Olive Senior *Summer Lightning and Other Stories* (London: Longman, 1986).

In this compelling collection of short stories Olive Senior vividly depicts the aspirations, hardships and fears of a rural Jamaican community in which family life is splintered by the constant barriers of class and colour. Her sensitive perceptions of childhood convey a private world of confusion and alienation, but also reveal a universal humanity observed with affection, poignancy and wit.

The collection is one of the most creative and exciting to emerge from the West Indies in recent times, and can be read fruitfully at secondary level.

D. The Treatment of Women / Women Characters

Although historically West Indian women were the repositories of folk wisdom and the oral tradition, they have only recently attempted or been able to project themselves in the written literature of the region. Thus whatever images of them appeared in the early literature were mostly images created by men in their preoccupation with appraisal and definition of the West Indian man. Since most of these appraisals concerned themselves with the evolution of West Indian man especially in relation to history, the images of women tended to concentrate on their historical role in this evolution. Historically the woman was central to the continuation of the slave system as a necessary part of the plantation system, her essential value resting on her ability to produce the labour force. This utilitarian and commercial view of her was only the planter's view however. In reality the slave woman was a mother in an almost spiritual sense. For her, the bond between mother and child was as sacred as the bond between the earth and creativity, and it was generally in her role as creator, protector and matriarch that early West Indian writers saw their spiritual survival. In the existing political ferment and self-assessments of the 1940s George Campbell portrayed Caribbean women in poetry as 'history makers', as 'women stone-breakers', as 'hammers and rocks' and as builders whose strength had provided not just the sustenance for survival but also the power to create a way of life and a sensibility.

The projection of the West Indian woman in literature has progressed from this image into various other images mostly in relation to the various historical and social changes in the region. It is possible for instance, to trace in Lamming's work alone a complex, interesting and historical view of the woman as she has progressed through West Indian history. There is first the image of the rural woman that appears in *In the Castle of My Skin,* the poor, hardy, often abandoned mother, lovingly committed to her child and to the land, uncritically optimistic and unquestioning of the *status quo,* but possessing a strength and a meaning derived from her sense of community and from the shared confidences and bonds between her and the people around her.

This image is later concretised and broadened in the image of Ma Shephard (in *Of Age and Innocence*) who becomes both a symbol of the earth and tradition and a conservative stumbling block in the way of radical transformation. Lamming's young boys in their commitment to freedom and resistance must ultimately reject her vision, and in *Season of Adventure* her spirit as embodied in the heroine has to be combined with her radical political vision. It is perhaps with a similar sense of the value and inadequacy of the rural woman's vision that Brathwaite evokes her consciousness in *Rights* only as part of a general progress towards a revolutionary will in *Islands.*

In other West Indian writers and even in Lamming himself, the image of the woman extends beyond the image of the earth mother. The very disintegration of rural life and the separations brought about by migrations and urban settlements created new priorities and ambitions and therefore new images of the woman. The picture of the rural woman in the urban world, bewildered and confused but doggedly set on making her way either as worker or prostitute, is a common image in West Indian urban novels. In De Lisser, Roger Mais and Orlando Patterson the image is deepened by a vision of her as doubly deprived and oppressed by society and by her men folk. In Patterson the aggressively ambitious urban prostitute, determined to move out of the dreary dunghill into a better life, is part of the novelist's general expression of the cycle of futility in which all slum dwellers are trapped. In Mais however, the degraded woman of the slum, for all her poverty and constriction, often possesses a generosity of spirit which is part of that communal spirit explored as a positive aspect of the slum world.

Ironically, very few West Indian women have specifically explored the social and psychological problems of women. In the 1940s the Jamaican poet Louise Bennett saw herself mostly as an oral performer and social commentator. Her social commentary was presented through the consciousness of her rural women, but it was mostly evocation and comment on the general social situation not exclusively on the women's situation. Thus she commented on women's view of marriage, on women's racial attitudes, and on women's strength and vulnerability in Jamaican society but mostly as part of a general social commentary. It is really only in writers like Merle Hodge, Jean Rhys, Erna Brodber and recently Grace Nichols that a certain particularised consciousness of the West Indian woman begins to emerge. For in all these writers the social world is evoked mostly through the consciousness of the women characters. In Hodge, the process of a little child's growth from childhood to maturity may well reflect a generalised preoccupation with West Indian problems of cultural confusion and identity but the little heroine's dilemmas about colour, prettiness and self-worth are also part of the tensions and confusions of a maturing female sensibility. In a similar sense Jean Rhys's *Wide Sargasso Sea* dramatises the ravaged status and the emotional alienation of the white creole woman from her West Indian background and at the same time reveals the dependence and vulnerability characteristic of all Rhys's female characters. In Brodber and Nichols the emphasis is more directly on the female experience. Nichol's evocation of the West Indian woman's evolution from slave to person is a celebration of the woman's struggles, fears, weaknesses and triumphs. *I is a Long Memoried Woman* evokes for the first time a total vision of the woman's progress, a vision which is a little removed from the 'earth mother' image especially in its very ambivalence towards the role of motherhood and in its radical revolutionary tone. In Brodber, it is mostly the contemporary woman's search for a personality and individuality amidst the various imprisoning roles imposed by small cramped societies that is highlighted. But on the whole the voice of the contemporary West Indian woman is yet to be established in the literature of the region. Very few women indeed write for a living in the West Indies, and the paucity of writers is perhaps a good explanation for the absence of a tradition of women's writing in the sense in which it exists for instance in Black American literature.

Major Texts

1. H.G. De Lisser *Jane's Career* (London: Methuen, 1914; Republished in Heinemann Caribbean Writers Series).

The novel contrasts the life of the woman in the rural and urban environments in Jamaica, concentrating on the young woman's vulnerability in the new grasping and exploitative Kingston environment. The heroine succeeds in the city, getting herself a husband, a house and, ironically, a servant.

2. George Lamming *In the Castle of My Skin* (London: Michael Joseph, 1953; Republished by Longman, London, 1979).

The women of Creighton Village, Barbados, are part of a pattern of existence and a vision of life which Lamming associates with an old order, with adjustments and sensibilities created in response to slavery, the colonial experience, and peasant life.

3. Edward Brathwaite 'The Dust', *Rights of Passage* (London: Oxford University Press, 1967).

In the voices of the folk women in 'The Dust' Brathwaite evokes the mind and sensibilities of the rural women, showing their apprehension of their environment and society, demonstrating their stoicism and resilience and identifying their cosmic understanding of time.

4. Merle Hodge *Crick Crack Monkey* (London: André Deutsch, 1970; Republished in Heinemann Caribbean Writers Series).

The heroine's divided consciousness and the insecurities that come with it are shown as a reflection of the racial and cultural conflicts in a young girl's upbringing.

5. Jean Rhys *Wide Sargasso Sea* (London: Hutchinson, 1966; Republished by Penguin Books, Harmondsworth, 1968).

The gradual dissociation between the heroine and the landscape, between her and the people she had always known, provokes a crisis of identity; her inability to cope with this as well as estrangement from her husband marks her out as vulnerable, the type of woman who in Rhys always becomes a victim.

6. Grace Nichols *I is a Long Memoried Woman* (London: Caribbean Cultural International, 1983; London: Karnak House Publication, 1983).

The poems celebrate the black woman's progress and evolution in the new world. They are the poet's imaginative rendering of the consciousness of the black woman as she has responded and adjusted to life in the West Indies.

7. Erna Brodber *Jane and Louisa will soon come Home* (London: New Beacon Books, 1980).

The novel deals with the contemporary woman's search for personality and self amidst the various imprisoning roles imposed on women in small societies.

8. Zee Edgell *Beka Lamb* (London: Heinemann, 1982).

The action of the novel only spans a short period in the life of the heroine but Edgell manages to suggest all those influences of church, home, school and the wider political world which help to shape the mind and outlook of a growing girl in the Belize of the mid-twentieth century.

9. Beryl Gilroy, *Frangipani House* (London: Heinemann Caribbean Writers Series, 1986).

Frangipani House won a prize in the GLC Black Literature Competition. Set in Guyana, it tells the story of Mama King who is trapped by age and infirmity. Her relatives send her to an institution from which Mama King eventually escapes, but not before she has been humiliated and driven to near madness. The book is a strong condemnation of institutions that deny respect to the old and weak.

E. The Theme of Migration

In West Indian literature the theme of migration has been a response both to an actual historical phenomenon and to a psychological problem created by colonial relations. At the turn of the century the decline of the sugar industry and of the importance of the West Indies heightened the constriction, poverty and isolation of the islands. Most West Indians genuinely felt hemmed in by the poverty and deprivations of their worlds and looked elsewhere for greener pastures, 'a better break' as most emigrants envisaged. In the early stages West Indians drifted to Panama where the building of the canal afforded opportunity for work and enrichment. Most migrants to Panama did return home however, often with money and new awarenesses, and West Indian literature has stories of the returned Panama migrant with his new flamboyant culture and his sharpened social awareness. Lamming's old man Pa (*In the Castle of My Skin*) recalls his own Panama days, and the author Eric Walrond recreates the exile's life in Latin America with compassion and depth in *Tropic Death* (1926). West Indian migration of the 40s and 50s was however mostly migration to England, and although like the drift to Panama this was also a search for a break, the entire phenomenon was complicated by the assumption of a shared heritage with the mother country. It was really the shattering of this illusion, of centuries of expectations fostered by colonial dependency and consolidated by a colonial education that led to the trauma and alienation so vividly recreated by novelists like Lamming and Selvon. Lamming's *The Emigrants* is for instance, a sombre and serious drama of the crumbling of the emigrant's illusions and of the alienation and personal disintegration that became his major experience in the metropolis. In *In the Castle of My Skin* Lamming's Trumper, the returned exile, posits a positive vision of exile and of the immigrant's experience as capable of fostering a sense of community and race and of enlarging the West Indian's vision of himself. In *The Emigrant* this is hardly realised. For if there is a sense of community on the ship that transports West Indian emigrants into England it is generated

49

only by a shared vulnerability and dependence. In the metropolis West Indian immigrants exist only on the periphery of mainstream British life, pushed there by a sense of exile and an irrelevance of function in a society whose past they cannot alter and whose future seeems always beyond them. The eventual fragmentation and isolation of the immigrant community only enact the drama of individual disconnection and alienation which Lamming sees as the emigrant's lot. Another dimension of the theme is explored in Lamming's examination of the West Indian artist's relationship to the situation of exile. For the three artists whose lives, work and relationships Lamming scrupulously delineates, the costs and perils of exile are measured in the bankruptcy of an artistic existence without a supporting community.

In Selvon the theme of emigration is much more humorously explored. While Lamming's immigrants appear in a perpetual sombre cage, Selvon's migrants are constantly outside, often on aimless fun-loving sprees but usually maintaining a sense of togetherness and community, a shared vocabulary and attitudes which make it possible for them to create their own 'portion' of England in spite of the wider loneliness they experience. Although the light-hearted tone often prevents a serious engagement and confrontation with the real psychological effects of disconnection and alienation, it establishes much more than Lamming does, a sense of West Indian presence, a warm and humane presence that often contrasts with the rigid coldness of their English neighbours. More recently the new generation of West Indians, British children of West Indian immigrants have added new tones, rhythms and dimensions to the theme. Where limited horizons, frustrations and unbelonging moved Lamming's characters to disintegration and set Selvon's on aimless sprees, these very pressures elicit harsh and angry rhythms from new generation poets like Linton Johnson and Bongo Jerry, moved partly by new conceptions of themselves not as immigrants but as deprived citizens.

The 'emigrant' experience outside the colonial metropolis presents interesting variations of theme. It would be worthwhile for instance to compare the experience of migration and exile in novels by Claude McKay (USA) Paule Marshall (USA) and

Austin Clarke (Canada) with the experience delineated by Lamming and Selvon. For there is a sense in which the emigrant's sojourn in the Americas is not complicated by the psychology of colonial relations and does not involve an intense shattering of illusions and expectations of a common heritage. Marshall's *Brown Girl, Brown Stones* is, for instance, more an attempt at reconciling a very strong Barbadian culture and consciousness with the demands of a different American culture, exploring as Austin Clarke also does, the conflicts and spiritual costs of this reconciliation.

Major Texts

1. Eric Walrond *Tropic Death* (New York: Bony and Liveright, 1926).

The stories in Walrond's collection dramatise the plight of West Indian migrants in search of work in Latin America. They evoke a grim picture of their squalid surroundings and their wretched lives. Set on the West Indian islands of the emigrants, on 'emigrant' ships and in Panama, the stories recreate a rounded picture of the 'nightmare' of migration.

2. George Lamming *The Emigrants* (London: Michael Joseph, 1954; Republished by Alison and Busby, London, 1980).

The novel is a drama of the West Indian's journey from the islands towards 'a better break' in England. The long drawn out nature of the journey and the claustrophobic atmosphere of the ship allows Lamming to explore the physical and psychological needs that motivate the emigrants and to relate them later to the realities of their existence in the metropolis.

3. George Lamming *Water With Berries* (London: Longman, 1971).

In this exhaustive exploration of the West Indian artist as an emigrant and immigrant Lamming measures the cost of exile not merely in terms of personal disintegration and alienation but also in terms of the deterioration of West Indian creative talent in the absence of a supporting community.

4. Edward Brathwaite 'The Emigrants', *Rights of Passage* (London: Oxford University Press, 1967).

Brathwaite's poem records the loss of real roots, and explores the diminution   involved in the experience of emigration. The sense of impersonality and invisibility which the emigrant experiences is for Brathwaite a bar to his full development as a person.

5. Samuel Selvon *The Lonely Londoners* (London: Wingate, 1956; Republished by Longman, London, 1972).

Selvon's novel treats with humour and comedy the West Indian immigrant life in England. Against a prevailing sense of their way of life back home Selvon explores their comic adjustments to new lives in England, revealing the conditions of their lives and their existence outside mainstream British life.

6. Samuel Selvon *Moses Ascending* (London: Wingate, 1975; Republished by Heinemann Caribbean Writers Series, London, 1984).

Selvon concentrates on the fortunes of a particular immigrant, recording his life after years of existence and struggle in England. The life story of Moses is really a reflection of the various stages in the West Indian immigrant's adjustment to life in England, a document of his social progress and personal awareness.

7. Linton Kwesi Johnson *Dread Beat and Blood* (London: Bogle L'ouverture Publications, 1975).

Linton Johnson's poems convey in angry and passionate tones the experience of the urban black in England. Created in the tradition of oral poetry they draw on the vernacular for both vocabulary and rhythm.

8. Claude McKay *Home to Harlem* (New York: Harper and Brothers, 1928).

McKay is mostly preoccupied with the black's existence and place in a predominantly white society. His Caribbean character, Ray, is the classic black intellectual tortured by a sense of alienation and feelings of unbelonging. His entire experience in the American city is a process of racial, social and political awareness.

9. Paule Marshall *Brown Girl, Brown Stones* (New York: Avon Books, 1959).

Paule Marshall's novel about Barbadian immigrants in Brooklyn explores the community's new life, expectations and ambitions in America against the background of their Barbadian culture, attitudes and rituals. Most of the dilemmas and conflicts in the novel dramatise the relationship between a strong Barbadian identity and the cultural demands of the new society.

10. Austin Clarke *The Bigger Light* (Boston & Toronto: Little Brown, 1975).

In this novel about Barbadian immigrants in Canada Clarke explores their cultural and personal alienation while at the same time showing their experience as a process of self-realisation and liberation.

F. The Rastafarian in West Indian Literature

Rastafarianism as an ideology has held an interest and a fascination for West Indian writers at various stages of the literature's progress. Various writers have projected the rastafarians' beliefs and rituals and featured their powerful speech rhythms in poetry and prose. In some respect this interest has been a response to the sense of self and dignity which the sect maintains through its very rejection of the imitative, bastardised version of 'British' society which most middle class West Indians consider the norm for their societies. It was really the strength and independence of mind behind their choice which fascinated a new generation of writers already dissatisfied with the mulatto self-image projected in earlier literature. Yet interestingly the rastafarians themselves could not be further away from the educated writers in background and upbringing. Products of Jamaica's urban life they were originally the dispossessed urban dwellers for whom Garvey's message of blackness and race pride had had a special meaning. For them the coronation of the Emperor Selassie in Ethiopia was nothing but the fulfilment of a prophecy made by their leader concerning the redemption of the African race from its bondage to the Western world. From this belief they created a new world and religion in which the Emperor became God, and Africa his promised kingdom on earth. As a sect, rastafarians grew steadily after the invasion of Abyssinia, becoming a mass movement that appealed mostly to the depressed of the slums and the dungle. As a sect they have featured in various dimensions in West Indian literature. In Mais's *The Hills Were Joyful Together* and *Brother Man* it is their humane philosophy of peace and brotherhood that is explored as a positive unifying force in the pinched and deprived world of the slum. For Orlando Patterson, writing in 1964, however, the rastafarians signified the very futility of transcending the depression and depravity of the dungle. Although in *The Children of Sisyphus* the fantasy about escape to Africa is obviously part of the rastafarian's rejection of his conditions and apart of his struggle to transcend them, Patterson presents it as part of the general absurdity of man's condition in the West Indies. But the very passion embodied in the rastafarian's dream of escape is motivated by an awareness of his squalid surroundings and of the deficiencies of the larger social world around him. This is the paradox that comes out in Brathwaite's portrait of him in 'Wings of a Dove' (*Rights*). For behind the rasta man's illusion of escape, behind the deadness and the labyrinth in which his perceptions are finally trapped, there is a clear sense of self and a true assessment of society, and these are what ultimately appeal to a poet in search of 'self' and vision, and in this respect Brathwaite sees an affinity between the rastafarian and the groping poet. Younger poets writing a few years after Brathwaite's *Rights* have suggested similar and subtle affinities between themselves and the rastafarian figure. Anthony McNeill has for instance, explored the ambiguities of the rasta man's dream of individual fulfilment as part of the ambiguities of the revolutionary consciousness, while in 'Sqatter's Rites' (*Uncle Time*) Dennis Scott has dramatised how his personal strength and dignity are reborn in his son's reggae music and celebrated in the very form of the poet's art. These perceptions and representations of the rastafarian are not just romantic views, they are part of the poet's recognition of the link between the rasta man's destiny and his own, and of the extent to which his own art demonstrates its responsibility to what he represents.

Major Texts

1. Roger Mais *The Hills Were Joyful Together* (London: Jonathan Cape, 1953; Republished in Heinemann Caribbean Writers Series)

Mais's novel evokes the pattern of life in the Jamaican slum yard, concentrating on its poverty, squalor and constriction and projecting their social consequences. On another level it explores the character of the community, revealing how the shared experience of poverty and deprivation can give rise to a sense of community and humanity and how the rastafarian, Ras, embodies some of these aspects.

2. Roger Mais *Brother Man* (London: Jonathan Cape, 1954; Republished in Heinemann Caribbean Writers Series).

The novel considers the possibilities that Mais hints at in *The Hills Were Joyful Together*. In the squalor, constriction and evil of the yard Mais explores the possibilities of messianic leadership as embodied in the spiritual vision of the rastafarian, Brother Man.

3. Orlando Patterson *The Children of Sisyphus* (London: New Authors, 1964).

Patterson's novel portrays rastafarianism as a social phenomenon of the Jamaican slum world and as an escape route for the deprived urban dweller anxious to overcome the conditions of his life. He presents the rastafarian's dream of escape especially in its relation to Africa as a sophisticated personal and spiritual escapism which is part of the general absurdity of man's condition in Jamaica.

4. Edward Brathwaite 'Wings of a Dove' *Rights of Passage* (London: Oxford University Press, 1967).

Brathwaite's poem reveals the paradoxes in the illusion behind the rastafarians' escapism and the social perceptions that give rise to it. His portrayal uncovers the clear sense of self and the perception of middle class rootlessness that inspire their dream of escape and rebellion.

5. Anthony McNeill 'Straight Seeking', 'Saint Ras', 'Ode to Brother Joe' in *Reel from 'The Life Movie'* (Kingston, Jamaica: Savacou, 1972).

All three poems are explorations of the rastafarians' significance to the poet. McNeill sees the passion of their dream as the quality that helps them to escape the crippling squalor of their surroundings. Although he mocks the illusion of the dream as he pits it against the stark details of the rasta's world, the poet recognises their passion and faith as contrasts to the general insensitivity of the larger Jamaican society.

6. Dennis Scott 'Squatter's Rites' *Uncle Time* (Pittsburgh: Pittsburgh University Press, 1973).

The poem is a celebration of the link between the rastafarian's condition and vision and the poet's art. The rasta's personal strength and vitality are reborn in his son's recognition and respect and in the reggae which he composes in his memory.

G. Post-Independence Critiques

In the West Indies the literature of the 60s and 70s was essentially a literature of disillusion and despondency. In contrast to the excitement and explosion of literary activity in the 30s and 40s, to the confidence and promise of the earlier nationalism, the 60s and 70s have been periods of pain, sorrow, despondence, silence and withdrawal. First the break up of the West Indian Federation in 1962 erased the wider notion of a West Indian political unit, leaving small nations for whom political independence was more a gift from the metropolis than an actively and independently worked achievement. Thus in the West Indies the aftermath of political freedom has been sadly ambiguous and most writers have reacted deeply to the very politics of freedom.

> is independence what it is? One day in July you say you want to be that there thing, an' one day in a next July the law say all right, from now you's what you askin' for. What change that can change? Might as well call your dog a cat an' hope to hear him mew. Is only words an names what don' signify nothin.

Most West Indian writers have echoed the disenchantment and cynicism of Lamming's character in *Season of Adventure,* for freedom has not brought self-knowledge and fulfilment, only the death of aspirations and the entrenchment of class and social barriers. Indeed in writers like Carter who had preached resistance and revolution in the 1950s the despondency has been more traumatic. For Carter lived through the Guianese racial divisions of 1957 and the race war of 1962-1964, and we have only to compare the fiery optimism of *Poems of Resistance* with the reticence and silence of Carter's later poetry to measure the extent to which the turn of politics had affected him. In 1963 when he wrote the poems in 'Jail Me Quickly', it seemed that he had lost the will to fight and had resigned himself to despair:

> Men murder men as men must murder men to build their shining Governments of the damned.

In the works of Walcott and Brathwaite a similar disenchantment with politics and the establishment was taking place. A great deal of the poems in the *Gulf* and *Sea Grapes,* for instance, attack the continuing (and indeed increasing) shallowness of the imitative society and in *The Star Apple Kingdom* and *The Fortunate Traveller* the tone of Walcott's political satire becomes increasingly sombre, due of course to a deepening cynicism about the course of politics and of political values in the region. In Brathwaite the attack on politics and society is embodied in the poet's dual apprehension of the society in general and in the dual vision of sterility and growth which informs the poet's perspective in poems like 'Homecoming', 'Trade Winds' and 'Pebble'. Brathwaite denounces 'the desert' of the political climate, the lack of vision, the exploitation of people and the seeming repetitiveness of history in the region:

> and the wheel turns
> and the future returns
> wreathed in disguises.

He balances this static fatalistic view with a sense of creative potential based on his sense of the poet's almost priestlike capacity to 'refashion futures' like a healer's hand. Even among younger poets like McNeill and Scott, the same bitter tones, the same violent denunciations of politicians, persist, confirming Lamming's recognition in *Season of Adventure* that independence in the West Indies had been hollow and purposeless.

In the novel the presentation of post-independence society has been similarly disenchanting. Naipaul who had already assessed West Indian potentiality in *The Mimic Men* continued to examine the capacity of post-colonial independence societies to restructure their societies. In *Guerrillas* his black power revolutionaries are portrayed as part of the disorder of a chaotic and decaying society, and their revolution becomes the response which each revolutionary makes to the disorder outside. Naipaul's conclusions about West Indian society are similar to his conclusions in *The Mimic Men* because the vision of society is historically determined. In this society, he concludes, self-assertion and revolution will always become a pose, part of the answer to the disorder outside. This view of the political and creative potential of the West Indies has been shaped by a vision of history that sees man as chained to his past and incapable of transcendence. But other writers of the region have conceived of a more fluid relationship between man and his past and have been able to envisage more open futures in which possibilities for re-fashioning futures exist. A novelist like Earl Lovelace who also explores the West Indian's potential for change and vision in *The Dragon Can't Dance,* appears more open in his exploration and less consumed by historical determinism and fatalism. Although Lovelace also questions the West Indian's capacity for revolution he locates the disability not in history *per se,* but in that loss of ritual and energy, that dissociation between West Indian man and his cultural and spiritual traditions that has created his paralysis and emptiness. Lovelace's perspective in *The Dragon,* the very metaphor of his explorations, establish the presence and potency of the rituals of carnival which his major characters stand in danger of bastardising and perverting. His portrayal of his characters' acts of rebellion which he presents as empty drama, find a link with that loss of ritual and energy which he symbolically dramatises in the major action of the novel. It is in the spiritual and moulding possibilities of carnival and dance that Lovelace locates possibilities. That is why *The Dragon Can't Dance,* for all its cynicism about revolution and change in the West Indies, is ultimately a novel of possibility.

Major Texts

1. Martin Carter 'Jail Me Quickly' *Poems of Succession* (London: New Beacon, 1977).

The poems appear to mark the climax of Carter's movement from the exhilaration of promise in the 1950s towards the trauma of political strife in the 60s and the resignation and fatalism which were his response to the failure of Guyana's political hopes. They comment on the political situation and on people and society, and the poet's tone moves from mockery towards a silent tragic resignation.

2. George Lamming *Season of Adventure* (London: Michael Joseph, 1960; Republished by Alison & Busby, London, 1979).

The novel is perhaps the first serious analysis of the failure of nationalism. It examines the quality of freedom and independence through its ruthless portrayal of the apparatus of power and of the shallowness and insecurity of the class that holds it. It is both an indictment of failure and an exploration of wholeness. The search for true freedom is linked with the search for identity, and both are explored in the heroine's relationship with her forgotten racial, historical and cultural self.

3. V.S. Naipaul *The Mimic Men* (London: André Deutsch, 1967; Republished by Penguin Books, Harmondsworth, 1970).

A portrait both of the society that achieves independence in the West Indies and of the people who hold political power. Naipaul relates the region's political possibilities to the society and its history and sees failure in the region's past and its present disorder.

4. V.S. Naipaul *Guerrillas* (London: André Deutsch, 1975).

In what appears to be Naipaul's ultimate statement on the West Indies the novel recreates the aspirations and slogans of the black power revolutionaries against the background of a decaying and chaotic West Indian society.

5. Edward Brathwaite *Islands* (London: Oxford University Press, 1969).

Poems like 'Homecoming' and 'Trade Winds' denounce the region's politicians not just for exploiting and violating the people but for depriving the entire region of a future. Brathwaite sees possibilities for 're-fashioning' futures not in the hands of politicians but in those of the poet, humble, sensitive and priest-like, yet close to the grounded folk.

6. Derek Walcott *Sea Grapes* (London: Jonathan Cape, 1976).

Walcott surveys and articulates the political climate of the Caribbean region through an artist's sensibility. His evocation and judgment centre on the ways in which the political climate affect the ordinary people. He sees the region's politicians as plodders without imagination, administering the last rites to their people; but the entire collection is informed by a vision of promise, of a vitality that is part of the creative resilience of the people, a power that can transform historical loss into promise.

7. Derek Walcott *The Star-Apple Kingdom* (London: Jonathan Cape, 1980; New York: Farrar, Straus & Giroux, 1979)

The collection is principally a political satire on Caribbean politics. It indicts the political leaders for failing to transform the region's potential. The poems take us on a journey through the archipelago, revealing the poet's deep disillusionment with the quality of life. In the 'Schooner Flight' the details of the protagonist's historical and contemporary experience explain his disillusion and exile. Delineated as a symbol and victim of corruption, his story becomes the story of the region's failure.

8. Mervyn Morris *Shadow Boxing* (London & Port of Spain: New Beacon, 1979).

In most of the poems in this collection Morris flays the various consciousness-raising movements that became a part of the social and political scene in the 60s and 70s: black power movements, political groups, grass roots movements. He presents these satiric themes through the consciousness of a folk character whose dialect-speaking voice reveals its own genuine natural wisdom as it uncovers the fraudulent poses of the new radical men.

9. Derek Walcott *The Fortunate Traveller* (London: Faber & Faber, 1982).

This collection is another critical evocation in which Walcott examines the relationship between the political apparatus and the quality of people's lives. Cleverly embodied in the point of view of a narrator and a calypsonian protagonist, it is a devastating exposure of the ineffectualness of government and of the distance, indifference and contempt with which politicians have always regarded the mass of the people in the West Indies.

H. Carnival

Trinidad's annual theatrical event though mainly distinguished now for its pageantry and fun is as old and singular as Trinidad's own history of settlement and slavery. This event which has grown to capture the entire Trinidadian imagination and become almost symbolic of a fun-loving West Indies ironically began as the annual entertainment of slave masters in eighteenth century Trinidad. For Carnival as an annual entertainment really began with the arrival in Trinidad of French speaking planter immigrants and their African slaves. A vigorous, fun-loving people, the French immigrants soon settled down to a free and comfortable life in what was then a mainly undeveloped and neglected outpost of the Spanish American Empire. Their Carnival, lasting from Christmas to Ash Wednesday, was a major season of diversion and entertainment, a season of uninhibited gaiety, of music, dance and masquerade during which as planters they could even permit themselves to fantasise about the slaves they held, to assume their roles, mask their costumes and dance their bamboulas and their ghombas and their kalindas.

Originally a leveller of barriers, Carnival grew to absorb rather than exclude other planter immigrants who flooded Trinidad during this time, and newcomers from the Spanish main and from the French and English islands easily found themselves a part of the yearly spectacle. The British conquest of Trinidad in 1797 encouraged a more stable development though it could not stop the flow of migrants and by the first half of the nineteenth century Trinidad's population had not only doubled but extended to include a diverse group of people and races. More slaves had been imported from Africa, and even after the abolition, slaves captured from slaving ships were almost always resettled in Trinidad. In this slave-based society of distinct groupings Carnival as an open entertainment was bound to be affected. The governing British administration introduced measures bringing it in line with the society's strict colour stratification. Slaves were excluded from the entertainment; free coloureds could participate only under stringent regulations, and the festival up until emancipation was a strictly white and free-coloured entertainment.   After the emancipation of slaves the existing stringent measures could not be effectively maintained. Freed slaves literally crashed into carnival entertainment taking their cue from plantation conditions and plantation life on the island. Planters had permitted themselves to fantasise about their slaves, masking their costumes and dancing their dances. Now freed slaves also took liberties and mocked the authority of the militia, staging mock battles, parodying the very authority which had wielded so much power over them. Such parodies, in addition to more traditional slave amusements at Christmas, became the frequent forms of diversion at Carnival time. The 'moko jumbie' on stilts and the 'John Canoe' in semi-military costume became regular sights at carnival processions, generating a new atmosphere of pre-Carnival meetings, rehearsals and get-togethers which still survive in the feverish pre-Carnival activities in the tents. Freed slaves, it appeared were taking over the Carnival. The street masquerades now had more and more scenes depicting aspects of slavery; street revellers were becoming noisier and noisier, and Carnival itself, as the white press saw it, was degenerating into a 'jamet carnival', an underworld affair and a relic of barbarism. In spite of several attempts the ruling class was never able to suppress this new thrust in Carnival entertainment. Every attempt met with more heightened resistance, and even occasional rioting from the mass of revellers. The annual celebration had become more like a symbol of freedom for them and was now, as Errol Hill observes,'no longer a European inspired nature festival but a deeply meaningful anniversary of deliverance with a ritualistic significance rooted in the very experience of slavery'. The new thrust naturally created its own rituals, and the procession of torches with which the planters had celebrated the beginning of Carnival became a vigorous procession of drumming and singing, while the 'camboulay' originally associated with Emancipation celebrations became a part of the Carnival 'Dimanche Gras' ritual, giving a distinctive significance to the freed slaves' appropriation of the festival.

The emergence of steel band music, itself a response to the official banning of drums and shacks provided Carnival with its special music just as the eventual rise of the professional

Calypsonian and the elaborate costumes and properties of the masquerade gave dimensions of theatre, spectacle and further ritual to the entire entertainment. Thus from its beginnings as a white planter-class diversion, Carnival progressed into a white and free-coloured upper-class entertainment; it was then appropriated by ex-slaves and the common people who made it into a ritual symbolic of their freedom and their uninhibited expression of themselves.

It is this essentially historical meaning of Carnival that is continually in danger of being overpowered by spectacle and theatre, and West Indian writers who have used aspects of Carnival as metaphors for expressing or commenting on West Indian realities have always hinted at this danger. Walcott's 'Mass Man' for instance, presents a double vision of Carnival as on the one hand a creative self-expression and on the other an excess of fantasy that obscures the real implications of the celebrations. His poet persona distances himself from the hedonism, fantasy and often cruel irresponsibility of Carnival revellers to project himself as the meditative poet who must stand back from fantasy and spectacle to draw out the significance of the festival.

> But I am dancing, look from an old gibbet
> my bull-whipped body swings, a metronome!
> Like a fruit-bat dropped in the silk cotton's shade
> my mania, my mania is a terrible calm.

In spite of his recognition of Carnival as an important folk expression, Brathwaite has expressed a similar ambivalence about people's relation to the festival. In *Islands,* the concluding section of his trilogy and the section particularly devoted to West Indian realities, Carnival becomes an important metaphor for the poet's examination of West Indian responses. The 'mass man' in 'Caliban' is depicted against a background of West Indian poverty and corruption and in an atmosphere of creative and political stalemate. His 'dance' which comes on in the second movement of the poem is, in this context, not a ritual celebration of the common man's freedom and self but a dance of escape, a descent into the 'limbo silence' of the self in a flight from the oppressiveness of the outer world. Carnival is thus not a medium of awareness and a spur to liberation but a deliberate blotting out of awareness and a rejection of the possibilities of regeneration. In 'Tizzic' Brathwaite's Carnival theme operates against the background of the ambiguity with which Tizzic himself is depicted. For, on the one hand, he is a folk character attuned to the soil and apparently liberated from bondage to slave master and plantation; yet on the other he is a man imprisoned in that irresponsible concept of manliness which the Calypsonian frequently celebrates in songs. His response to the ritual and music of Carnival is governed by his own personal contradictions, and the ceremony is for him both a source of contact with

> days of green unhur-
> ried growing

and an escapist dream of heaven that momentarily obliterates the impoverished and confusing present. Carnival is thus not a medium of spiritual regeneration for him but a temporary vision of glory which after its 'blazing apotheosis' returns Tizzic to the real world, to Lenten sorrows, Ash Wednesday, 'ashes, darkness, death.'

It is perhaps only in the closing section of Brathwaite's *Islands* that Carnival becomes a metaphor of illuminations and a realistic summing up and acceptance of the processes of life in the West Indies. For the poem 'Jou'vert', signifying the morning of Carnival, celebrates neither the escapist prancing and 'limbo descent' of Caliban's carnival nor the borrowed glory of Tizzic's uplift. Its music and dance recall rather the losses and gains of history: the upheavals and displacements ('cries of arrows', 'lightening flashes', 'men asunder') the transformations, the compromises and the new fragile adjustments; the 'sorrows' burning to 'ashes', 'grey rocks' melting to 'pools'.

> of lashes'
> sweat and flowers

Dawn rides over 'shattered homes',

> and furrows
> over fields

and musty ghettos
over men now

hearing
waiting

watching
in the Lent-

en morning
hurts for-

gotten, hearts
no longer bound

to black and bitter
ashes in the ground.

Thus without saying it in as many explicit words, Brathwaite's final image of Carnival reiterates its historical roots as an affirmation and celebration of a people's sense of becoming.

In *The Dragon Can't Dance* Earl Lovelace not only returns us to the historical roots of Carnival but also explores its meaning and significance in a twentieth century post-war situation. Carnival becomes both subject and metaphor as he portrays his slum world and delineates its attempts at creating a visibility. Using the festival as both metaphor and form he dramatises its potential as a ritual for regeneration and self assertion while at the same time exploring its meaning and significance for the deprived characters of the slum. Thus, on the one hand, we get the whole ritual of Carnival: the song and dance, the shout, the costume and the masquerade jump, celebrations of the self; and on the other, the novelist's careful scrutiny of the nature of that self. Lovelace implies throughout that Carnival must go beyond the ritual shout, that finally each generation must interpret it in terms of its particular social and political situation and needs. The 'mass man's' Dragon dance in the novel fails as an assertion of a meaningful self because it never moves beyond the pose of terror and menace, beyond the religion of idleness which had signified rebellion among emancipated slaves in an earlier age. Thus in spite of the faith, the memories and the effort of creativity, the mass man's dragon succeeds only in drawing attention to itself. The novel's organisation works towards this illumination, and the 'dragon' recognises at last the limitations of his masquerade dance.

In other West Indian works Carnival is often simply evoked as a folk festival to which characters respond either positively or negatively according to their peculiar social and psychological problems. Merle Hodge for instance, uses Carnival as part of a world and a way of life to which her protagonist responds with embarrassment and ambivalence. Tee's response is dramatised as part of her 'middle-class' embarrassment about the folk but her spontaneous enjoyment of the yard scene is the author's subtle suggestion that the festival is part of her legacy.

Carnival as a folk form has evidently captured the imagination not just of the mass man and pan man but also of those writers working with the 'written' form. This interplay between the oral and the written form is a significant and unique aspect of West Indian literature and is eventually what would define the distinctiveness of the entire literature.

Major Texts

1. Edward Brathwaite 'Caliban' *Islands* (London: Oxford University Press, 1969).

Brathwaite's portrait of the masquerade dancer points to the dance's potential for spiritual regeneration, but Caliban prefers the dance of escape, the dance or descent into self as a means of obliterating an oppressive present.

2. Edward Brathwaite 'Tizzic' *Islands* (London: Oxford University Press, 1969).

Like Caliban's 'mass' Tizzic's carnival dance is also an escape. Caliban descends into the limbo silence of the self; Tizzic ascends an imagined and borrowed heaven. Both fail to exploit the potential of the 'mass' and the dance.

3. Edward Brathwaite 'Jou'vert' *Islands* (London: Oxford University Press, 1969).

In this final section of *Islands,* Brathwaite gives a positive vision of Carnival and points to its potential as catharsis and affirmation. Here the dance is an understanding and illumination rather than an escape. In its vision of the processes of history and of the adjustments and transformations of the West Indies, it becomes both catharsis and a dance of affirmation.

4. Earl Lovelace *The Dragon Can't Dance* (London: André Deutsch, 1979, Longman Drumbeat, 1981; Republished by Longman, London, 1981).

A novel that explores the meaning of Carnival to the deprived masses of the city's backyard. Lovelace examines the popular concept of warriorhood in relation to rebellion. His 'mass men' see themselves as warriors shouting a self but Lovelace's drama flays both the meaning and value of that self.

5. Merle Hodge *Crick Crack Monkey* (London: André Deutsch, 1970; Republished in Heinemann Caribbean Writers Series).

A novel that dramatises a growing girl's confusion in the class and cultural chaos of twentieth century Trinidad. Hodge's heroine walks in two worlds, one that is open, natural and unsophisticated but warm and comforting, and another that is polished but stilted and unsure. The heroine's response to Carnival becomes a mirror of her inner conflict and her divided self.

6. Derek Walcott 'Mass Man' *The Gulf* (London: Jonathan Cape, 1969).

A poem in which Walcott defines his relationship to Carnival and at the same time distances himself from its excesses and its degeneration. The poem depicts both the creativity and spectacle of the festival and the loveless, often cruel, abandon of the general mass of revellers. Walcott projects himself as the poet isolated by the mindless gaiety of the people and therefore able to draw out the real historical significance of the ceremony.

7. Wilson Harris, *Carnival* (London: Faber and Faber, 1985).

Carnival is a modern Dantesque allegory which confronts indigenous and metropolitan worlds to explore the possibilities of change in a violence-ridden universe. By fusing his own version of West Indian carnival and Dantesque allegory, Harris actualizes in his own narrative the marriage of cultures they achieve.

I. The Calypso

The calypso is part of a tradition of verbal arts and biting commentary in the West Indies, and is historically linked to the post-emancipation 'takeover' of Carnival, first by freed slaves and later by the urban folk in the city's yards. The gradual transformation of Carnival created in its wake a variety of forms and expressions which helped to make the Calypso what it is today. Freed slaves celebrated Carnival not with ballroom dances and promenades but with songs, street dancing, drumming and stick fighting, creating a general street theatre which gave ample opportunities for free and open expressions and for uninhibited abuse and criticism. Songs of comment and abuse were part of this theatre and were often directed both at rival groups of revellers and at the authority of the ruling class. Each lead singer drew up his own chorus of singers to complete the yearly street drama, and the Carnival songs normally emerged spontaneously from these street contracts and provocations. Association with the yearly Carnival led to more planning and preparation and to the composition of special songs to match the themes of the masquerade bands; and though these preparations generally reduced possibilities for spontaneous compositions and improvisation they created a social setting and framework as well as a regular audience. With such regular appearances in Carnival tents, the lead singer (Calypsonian) became a performer with costume, gestures and song, and the tents themselves became platforms for an often creative interpretation between performers and an increasingly knowledgeable and discriminating audience.

Trinidadians value verbal expertise. For them the way a thing is said is always very important and in these performances Trinidadians judged Calypsonians not just for the melody of their song but also for their lyrics, for the quality of comment and the measure of verbal manipulation they employed in delivering it. The good and popular Calypsonian therefore, always composed in the context of the audience's assumptions and vocabulary but manipulated these to make judgements and criticisms, presenting these in a lyric powerful enough to stretch their imaginations as well.

In the course of time, frequent performances by lead singer and band led to the formation of special bands which performed throughout the year, but became especially active at Carnival time when Calypsos were composed around the general theme of Carnival bands. The lead singer of the band emerged into the Calypsonian of today, and the entire tradition of song, comment and provocation became part of an urban sub-culture. The Calypso itself grew to become a distinctive form, capturing and interpreting aspects of Trinidad's oral forms, mostly the 'lime', the 'old talk' and the 'picong', and evolving special canons by which its practitioners could be appreciated and judged. Certain characteristics came to be accepted as peculiar to the Calypso, so that often, beneath the veil of jolliness and levity suggested both by the music and the performance, the Calypso contained (for instance) a great deal of incisive social observation and commentary. The Calypsonian constantly monitored what was happening around him and used his songs and the platform of the tents to make social comments and expose wrong-doings and misdemeanour. His Calypso's point of view was often a combination of his own judgement and the judgement of the man in the street, and his pose nearly always the pose of the by-stander, the observer left to sift out a message and deliver conclusions. Very often he crystallised a general mood about a situation long before the general public had time to verbalise these and it is really because of this special relationship to events in society that commentators are now able to trace Trinidad's social and political history from a critical analysis of Calypsos composed over a period of years. For commentary in the Calypso ranges from the early jingoistic songs of the nationalist period (when Calypsonians sang in praise of a stable, happy and racially harmonious Trinidad) to the later satires and bitter presentations of the often sordid realities of politics and society on the island. The political satires often derived from two sources: from the clash between the politicians' own self-image and the Calypsonian's depiction of it, and from the jarring effects of those songs of attack couched in the form of earlier jingoistic

Calypsos. Sparrow's 'Model Nation' and Sniper's 'Portrait of Trinidad', earlier Calypsos composed in this tradition were, for instance, satirised in Black Stalin's 'New Portrait of Trinidad' sung in the same mode but with different images and completely opposite effects.

But generally speaking, the Calypsonian is more of a social commentator than an outright political satirist and his Calypsos not only create a particular social view-point but also occasionally reflect some of the society's own obsessions, contradictions and ambivalences. There is for instance, a whole tradition of calypso composition that specialises in the consistent bloating of a male super-ego and in the embarrassment and degradation of women. The Calypsonian very often celebrates male ego by depicting a sexually dominant male figure, often irresponsible and immoral but always strong, triumphant and eventually 'heroic'. The female figure is almost always at the butt end of this type of Calypso and she is often embarrassed, humiliated and finally rejected by an exultant male. Such depictions, rendered powerfully humorous by the Calypsonian's dexterity with language and rhythm, always raises instant laughter, but the real Calypsonian, the man of substance, always attempts to move beyond this humour, to project himself as the commentator, poet and conscience of his society.

The Calypso features in West Indian literature as both theme and form, and there is a sense in which its special techniques as a folk and oral form have helped to give shape to a number of West Indian imaginative works. There is in West Indian literature what we can call a 'Calypso style', usually involving a certain way of presenting a situation and a particular way of manipulating both language and 'audience'. For as an oral folk form, the Calypso has always worked with the language as it is spoken and with social and cultural assumptions shared by both Calypsonian and audience. Usually, as in the prose narratives of Selvon and Lovelace, the rhythms of the spoken word are captured in prose narrative; well-known images are manipulated and combined with the favourite aside, 'the lime', 'old talk' and the popular joke, giving prose narrative the flavour of a Calypso song. All the episodes in Selvon's *Lonely Londoners* are presented in this way and within the creole language without the intrusions of 'standard' English so that each episode becomes a kind of 'oral delivery' in itself. In *A Brighter Sun* where standard English and the creole language operate together, the 'calypso style' is incorporated into those sections where Selvon leaves his characters on their own to 'deliver' their responses to people and situations in their own creole language and within the framework of assumptions they share with other characters and with the readers. For Lovelace, the Calypso is interestingly both language and movement and is enacted especially in *The Dragon Can't Dance* as both music and dance. The Calypso effect is achieved chiefly through the manipulation of structure and rhythm, for Lovelace's sentences enact the actual rhythms and movements of the Calypso dance, projecting its function as purgation and catharsis:

> There is dancing in the Calypso. Dance! Dance to the hurt! Dance! If you catching hell, dance, and the government don't care, dance! Your woman take your money and run away with another man, dance! Dance! Dance! Dance!

As subject and theme the Calypso has functioned in West Indian literature as a depiction of an aspect of West Indian life, and Calypsos have often been evoked to illustrate and confirm observations and judgements held by the general mass of the population. In certain instances, as in Naipaul's *Miguel Street,* the Calypso is evoked both as social commentary and as caustic satire, because often the very consciousness that its observations and judgements confirm is the consciousness that Naipaul exposes as a negative manifestation of slum life. Often the levity and irresponsibility that lurk beneath the Calypso's melody reflect similar qualities in the characters themselves and the similarity explains their continual wish to be linked to those made popular in the Calypso.

In other West Indian works, the Calypso theme features as delineations of the Calypsonian and a dramatisation of the potency, power and traps of his craft. A.J. Seymour's poem 'To a Calypso Singer' and Edward Brathwaite's poem 'Calypso' both suggest the possibilities and the dangers. Seymour sees the Calypso becoming an opium for inertia, a substitute for radical thought and action; Brathwaite manipulates his poem to suggest a seriousness that goes beyond the Calypsonian's flippant and superficial view of the islands. It is perhaps only in *The Dragon Can't Dance* that we are given a full portrait of a Calypsonian. Lovelace's Philo is by far the most detailed study of a Calypsonian in West Indian literature, and his career dramatises the economic necessity and the spiritual impoverishment that lead to the degeneration of the Calypsonian and his craft. Philo's predicament is shown as finally not his alone but as equally the predicament of a society that has lost track of the values of its forms and compromised with mediocrity.

Major Texts

1. V.S. Naipaul *Miguel Street* (André Deutsch, 1959; Reprinted by Penguin Books, Harmondsworth, 1974).

A collection of stories in which Naipaul depicts the character, mentality and values of people in an urban backyard.

Relevant Stories

'The Thing Without a Name'

In Naipaul's *Miguel Street* the values that people uphold are not the values that foster ambition and uplift and Naipaul uses the Calypso's themes to reinforce this negative attitude. The Calypso that immortalises Popo is a Calypso that sings of his jail sentence. When Popo acts responsibly he is shunned as an outsider. When he returns to the fold and becomes a criminal his 'reputation' is re-established and the street proudly links itself to the Calypso that sings of his crime.

'The Coward'

A story that gives an ironical portrait of the street's 'bad John', a man for whom Carnival and street band are like ritual and religion. The Calypso is his main source of reference and he lives its words, becomes the bully and terror of the street though inwardly he is a frightened little man.

'The Pyrotechnist'

The Calypso functions here in a rather negative way. Naipaul points to its tendency to trivialise what is serious. Morgan tries all his life to be a comedian, to stir up laughter. When he finally succeeds it is for something not at all funny.

'The Maternal Instinct'

Here the Calypso becomes a point of reference supporting Nathaniel's sadistic attitude towards women. In this story the degradation of women is only a pose, fulfilling the street's concept of manliness. Ironically it is Nathaniel himself who is beaten by his woman.

'Caution'

The only story which celebrates Calypso as a spontaneous creative act. News of the end of the war and of the coming peace brings on a Carnival and a Calypso 'springs out of nothing'. But the song that comes out is negative, titillating and unrelated to the 'peace'.

'Until the Soldiers Come'

The story dramatises the impact of the Americans on the values of the people in Trinidad. The Calypso's observations about the American take-over is acted out.

2.   Edward Brathwaite 'Calypso' *Rights of Passage* (London: Oxford University Press, 1967).

Dramatises the violence of the island's history which the Calypsonian deflates in his flippant and superficial portrayal.

3. Earl Lovelace. *The Dragon Can't Dance* (London: André Deutsch, 1979; Reprinted by Longman, London, 1981).

Depicts the degeneration of the Calypso singer, pressed by economic necessity to cheapen and popularise an essentially serious talent.

Part 2: Black British Literature

Section 1: Introduction

A Traditions and Contradictions: The propaganda of 'otherness'

In June 1948 the *S.S. Empire Windrush* docked at Tilbury, and 492 Jamaicans disembarked upon England, their Motherland. Between that date and today, several hundred thousand West Indians, Africans and Asians came to live in Britain. The Empire was coming 'home', claiming their rights of abode as British citizens holding British passports. Although in this period of emigration, several hundred thousand white non-British people were accepted for settlement in Britain (Poles, Eastern Europeans, Ukranians and other nationalities displaced by the Second World War, for instance), popular and official hostility has been directed overwhelmingly against the black immigrants. New political parties with popular appeal arose to campaign for the repatriation of blacks. The National Front and other extreme and violent right-wing organisations won sizeable support in local and national elections. The mainstream parties - Labour and Conservative - passed Acts of Parliament designed to restrict and then terminate the flow of black Commonwealth immigration. A Nationality Act was passed which redefined the concept of 'nationality' so as to further limit the black presence in Britain. All these measures can be seen as a profound reversal of British and European historical tradition. Traditionally, Europe observed and practised total freedom of movement with regard to territorial boundaries. Hence for instance three continents of the world (North America, South America, Australia), which a few centuries ago belonged wholly to indigenous peoples are now overwhelmingly populated by European immigrants and their descendants. The native peoples have mostly been exterminated to make way for the European immigrants. Things have changed, however, and Britain, although still fiercely proud of its traditions, has shown itself willing to neglect the odd one.

The Jamaican immigrants who came on the S.S. *Empire Windrush* in 1948 were obeying traditions. West Indians, historically, have only travelled to work. Between the seventeenth and early twentieth centuries, they had been shipped from Africa and India to the West Indies to work in the plantations. In the period up to the Second World War, they were recruited to build the Panama canal and to work in the factories of the United States of America. After the Second World War there was great demand in Britain as the nation began to rebuild her broken cities. West Indians were actively recruited to work, through advertisements placed in West Indian journals by London Transport, the British Hotels and Restaurants Association, and similar organizations. They came to work in factories, buses, trains, hotels and hospitals, in jobs traditionally of low status and low pay. And they came with a sense of cultural identification with the Motherland. They saw themselves as British. Their education after all was based on the British system: the books they read (from the *Royal Reader* to Enid Blyton and William Wordsworth) were books being taught in schools in Britain. Their language was English or English-based; their religions (Church of England, Methodist, Presbyterian, etc.) were derived from Britain and passed on to them by British missionary movements. And the very towns, villages and counties they lived in were named after British places and personalities - for instance, Georgetown, Albion Estate or Brighton village (in British Guiana); Cornwall, Middlesex, Surrey (counties in Jamaica); Barbados, with its Nelson's Column at the heart of its capital (the Column with its statue of Lord Nelson predating the one in London's Trafalgar Square) was commonly known as 'Little England'. The journey to Britain however was a journey to an illusion, for the West Indian immigrants faced the reality of rejection by the Motherland. They may have believed passionately in their closeness and affinity to Britain and possessed a sense of belonging, but the British were equally convinced of their alienness, their otherness. In May 1953 Mr. Beresford Craddock, Member of Parliament, rose from his seat in the House of Commons to give his opinion of black people:

> Let us remember that 95 per cent of them are primitive people. One of the reasons why they are not generally accepted into hotels is because their sanitary habits are not all that could be desired ... It is well known that a large number of Africans in East and Central Africa are riddled with a disease of a very unfortunate kind ... I will not dwell on that very delicate subject, but I think that Hon. Members who have experience will agree that the attitude of the African towards women and sexual matters is entirely different from the attitude of the general run of Europeans ... it is a common practice among Africans to put children to sleep by the excitation of their erogenital organs ... The effect of alcohol upon an African is remarkable. I admit that sometimes alcohol has a remarkable effect on Europeans. But, speaking generally, alcohol seems to bring out all the evil instincts in the African in the most astonishing way ... these views and practices are due to the psychological make-up of those primitive people from time immemorial.

Craddock's declaration was official expression of common British recoil from black people, an attitude which defined them as alien beings, naturally different from British racial stock. British politicians, echoing popular sentiment, have tended to emphasise 'otherness', 'alienness' and 'difference', as if Blacks belonged to a separate category of the human species. Take for example Enoch Powell's speech in September 1971:

> Of the great multitude, numbering already two million, of West Indians and Asians in England, it is no more true to say that England is their country than it would be to say that the West Indies, or Pakistan, or India are our country. In these great numbers they are, and remain, alien here as we would be in Kingston or Delhi; indeed, with the growth of concentrated numbers, the alienness grows, not by choice but by necessity.

Again, the stress on the 'alienness' of the newcomers. In January 1978 Margaret Thatcher, now Prime Minister of Britain, continued in this tradition, in her notorious speech, broadcast on prime-time television, about British culture being swamped by aliens:

> If we went on as we are, then by the end of the century there would be 4 million people of the New Commonwealth or Pakistan here. Now that is an awful lot and I think it means that people are really rather afraid that this country might be swamped by people with a different culture. And, you know, the British character has done so much for democracy, for law, and done so much throughout the world, that if there is a fear that it might be swamped, people are going to react and be rather hostile to those coming in.

This philosophy, expressed by politicians, regarding the 'alienness' of the Blacks was, indeed, translated into violent popular action to expel them from the 'host body'. In August 1948, two months after the arrival of the S.S. *Empire Windrush* a white crowd of between 2-300 people gathered outside an Indian restaurant in Liverpool and set upon a West African customer, damaging the premises extensively. The next day, a crowd of 2,000 whites attacked Colsea House, a hostel in Liverpool for black seamen. A decade later, in the summer of 1958, anti-black riots erupted in Nottingham and in the Notting Hill area of London, with gangs of white teenagers engaged in 'nigger hunting'. Petrol bombs, stones, broken bottles and knives were the weapons used. By the end of August 1958, brawls, disturbances and racist attacks were a daily and nightly feature of life in north Kensington. The troubles spread to Kensal Green, north Paddington, Harlesden, Southall, Hornsey, Islington, Hackney, Stepney and out of London to towns like Middlesborough. As one immigrant put it, 'a black man's treated worse than a dog here', his statement revealing the way the humanity of black people was at peril, both physically and conceptually.

B. The emergence of black British writing.

Among the immigrants from 1948 onwards were young writers (Sam Selvon, V.S. Naipaul, Wilson Harris, George Lamming, Roger Mais and others) many of whom had already published work in the West Indies but who needed the resources of the metropolis to survive as writers and to gain wider recognition. The great publishing houses were in England, capable of supporting a writer financially and distributing his/her work throughout the world. But these practical considerations apart, the writer from the colonies felt a need and duty to represent colonial societies, to reveal the humanity of the people to a British society maliciously ignorant of that humanity. The urgent task was to address and convince a British readership of the human values that resided in black communities. The writer was thus a missionary in reverse, coming to Britain to educate and civilize the ignorant. 'What I have attempted', Vic Reid wrote in the Preface to his novel *New Day*, 'is to transfer to paper some of the beauty, kindliness and humour of my people, weaving characters into the wider framework of these eighty years and creating a tale that will offer as true an impression as fiction can of the way by which Jamaica and its people come today.'

This burden of revelation is characteristic too of earlier black writing in Britain, for black British literature is not a modern phenomenon. In eighteenth century Britain slave narratives and autobiographies were published by writers like Equiano, Gronniosaw and Cugoano, all of which yield unique insights into black existence, and which make strong appeals to the European reader to recognise the humanity of the African. Equiano for instance, in his autobiography, describes Africa, remembered from childhood days, as a land of musicians, poets and craftsmen, with systems of trade, with laws and codes of civilized behaviour. Equiano, in these descriptions of his people is consciously retaliating against the racist attitudes of eighteenth century Britain. British travel books, essays, poetry and fiction represented Africa overwhelmingly as the heart of darkness. Africans were described as a backward people, more animal than human, their relation to the human species being a matter of doubt. Samuel Estwick for instance pronounced on their 'otherness', claiming that they 'differed from other men, not in *kind,* but in species'. Thomas Atwood focusses on Africa's inability to produce artists and scientists:

> There is ... something so very unaccountable in the genius of all negroes, so very different from that of white people in general, that there is not to be produced an instance in the West Indies, of any of them ever arriving to any degree of perfection in the liberal arts or sciences, notwithstanding the greatest pains taken with them.

Lord Chesterfield is even more blunt in his equating of Africans and savage beasts. Africans to him are 'the most ignorant and unpolished people in the world, little better than lions, tigers, leopards, and other wild beasts, which that country produces in great numbers'. As in the post *Empire Windrush* period, there were frequent calls in the eighteenth century for the deportation of blacks who had been brought to Britain to work in the households of returning West Indian planters and merchants. The *Daily Journal* of 5th April 1723 reported on white anxieties about black immigration:

> 'Tis said there is a great number of Blacks come daily into this City, so that 'tis thought in a short Time, if they be not suppress'd, the City will swarm with them.

Equiano's generation of British blacks experienced the same rejection and hostility as today's generation. White British people have exhibited and sustained a remarkable resistance to black people living in their midst over three centuries. Today's generation of black writers voice anger and alienation, in a way that recalls the narratives of eighteenth century slaves, and reminds us of the enduring myth of 'difference' and 'otherness'.

Our study focusses almost exclusively on the poetry produced by today's generation of writers since the overwhelming bulk of the new literature consists of poetry. In addition, the black British literature most easily available to students and teachers are books of poetry. A few novels are beginning to appear, by David Simon, Janice Shinebourne, Caryl Phillips and others, and there is a sprinkling of dramatists, the most noteworthy being Edgar White. The major literary thrust however is in the mode of poetry. None of the present novelists and dramatists have as yet made any significant innovative impact on the language or form of the novel or drama, whereas the poets have used language and form in startlingly radical ways. The last great innovator in British poetry this century has been T.S. Eliot. It may well be that when the history of twentieth century British poetry comes to be written up, the black poets will be recognised for greatly enriching poetic expression through their experiments with orality and music.

Section 2: Notion of 'otherness' in British literature on blacks.

To understand the significance of black British literature, it is necessary to evaluate it against the mass of white British literature, from the seventeenth to the twentieth century, which depicts blacks in a variety of ways. Black British writers in their attempt to refine and redefine notions of self, react deliberately or unconsciously, against the images of white literature. The following are representative white texts which, appearing at various stages in the creation of the British Empire, throw light upon the shifting attitudes to black people over the centuries. What emerges from such a study is a realization of the ways in which black people have been fodder for white concept-ualization. Their social, personal and historical realities are constantly ignored or denied. They are instead creatures of myth, the demons or buffoons of the white imagination, the personification of notions of savage or exotic 'otherness'.

A. Shakespeare's *Titus Andronicus* (c. 1590-1592)

Elizabethan dramatists derived their information on Africa partly from travel books, which were published in the sixteenth century; many of them were then collected together in a monumental publication by Richard Hakluyt in 1589 and 1598 entitled *The Principal Navigations, Voyages and Discoveries of the English Nation*. Hakluyt's compilation had a profound and exhilarating impact on the Elizabethan imagination: the travel literature contained descriptions of the marvels and curiosities of newly discovered lands and alien culture wholly different from the world of Europe. The blackness, nakedness and 'heathen' religious, social and sexual practices of Africans were matters of excited speculation and horror. Blackness of skin was a badge of sin and shame, a result of God's curse on Ham, the son of Noah. The nakedness of the Africans was deemed to be a token of their promiscuity and sensuality. Black women were said to have mated with apes, and the men were lecherous and monstrous in their appetites. Richard Eden summarized such attitudes in 1555 when he described Africans as 'a people of beastly living, without a god, law, religion or commonwealth' (by 'commonwealth', Eden meant 'social systems').

These concepts about black people were absorbed into Elizabethan drama and personified in figures like Muly Mahomet and Eleazor (black characters in Thomas Peele's *The Battle of Alcazar*, c. 1588, and Thomas Dekker's *Lust's Dominion or the Lascivious Queen*, c. 1599). Muly Mahomet is a cruel, barbaric creature steeped in slaughter:

> Black in his look and bloody in his deeds
> And in his shirt stained with a cloud of gore.

He murders his uncle and his relations so as to claim the throne of Barbary. He delights in plotting and drawing up schemes for murder and mayhem. For much of the play he raves and froths, a torrent of curses pouring forth from his mouth. Eleazor is also a cunning monster, plotting and scheming with his lover to slaughter their way to power, and attempting to rape his lover's daughter. In his indecencies he behaves like the African 'savages' described in travel literature.

Sometime between 1590 and 1592, a new play by William Shakespeare, entitled *Titus Andronicus* was performed in London, having a black man - a Moor called Aaron - as one of its central characters. The play is a gruesome affair, replete with slaughter and cannibalism - it is a pot-boiler in the sense that it was a popular revenge thriller written to make easy money; a pot-boiler too in the sense that some of the characters in the play end up being cooked and eaten. The story is of Titus Andronicus, a noble Roman general returning to Rome after a heroic and triumphant campaign against the Goths. He brings with him trophies of war and a train of captives, including Tamora, Queen of the Goths, her sons, and her Moorish slave, Aaron. The Emperor of Rome is seduced by Tamora's beauty, and he marries her. She begins to plot revenge against Titus Andronicus. Titus's daughter is repeatedly raped, then mutilated by Tamora's two sons (her tongue and hands are cut off). Titus's two sons are falsely implicated in a murder and beheaded. Titus himself is deceived into chopping off his hand as a gift to placate the wrath of the Emperor. The stage therefore is populated with characters stumbling about, with stumps for legs and arms, and dripping blood. Some of the stage directions indicate the comic gruesomeness of the play. Act 2, Scene 4 opens, 'Enter Lavinia, her hand cut off, her tongue out, and ravished'; or Act 3, Scene 1: 'Enter a Messenger, bearing two heads and a hand'. Titus Andronicus gets his revenge: he kills Tamora's two sons, chops them up, boils them, and serves them up as pies at a banquet attended by Tamora. After Tamora has dined well on the pies, Titus reveals all, Tamora naturally chokes and splutters and throws up, and Titus stabs her to death.

The agent of death and the instigator of all these mutilations is none other than Aaron, the black man. It is Aaron who incites Tamora's sons to rape Titus's daughter, and it is Aaron who engineers the frame-up and execution of Titus's two sons. He revels in chaos: he is described as 'chief architect and plotter of these woes'. He enjoys murder and boasts of his evil:

> O how this villany
> Doth fat me with the very thoughts of it!
> Let fools do good, and fair men call for grace,
> Aaron will have his soul black like his face.

At his *first* entrance he launches into a long monologue, full of schemes and foul plots and declarations of wicked intentions; in his *last* speech, when he is sentenced to death, he is totally unrepentant; he curses them all and leaves the stage swearing murder. Such evil fury is typical of his outbursts:

> Vengeance is in my heart, death in my hand
> Blood and revenge are hammering in my head

In the play Aaron's black skin is indicative of his evil soul: his blackness is both physical and moral. His blackness is also a badge of sexual lust. He is Tamora's lover. Tamora - the Queen of Goths and Empress of Rome - is infatuated by him. She is herself something of a nymphomaniac, 'a most insatiate and luxurious woman'. Tamora becomes pregnant, has a child by Aaron - dangerous, since the child is black, and Tamora had passed off the pregnancy as being the result of her marriage to the Emperor. Tamora, as soon as the baby is born (which is described as 'a joyless black and sorrowful issue') gives it to Aaron to be killed, but Aaron refuses, and curses the whites for their colour prejudice: 'Is black so base a hue?', he asks, asserting that 'coalblack is better than another hue'. He touchingly defends the child against attempts to murder it, and makes a deal with Lucius, Titus Andronicus's son, whereby he would expose Tamora, in return for assurances that his baby will not be harmed. Aaron's sensitivity to his colour, and defence of his colour, reveal the extent of colour prejudice in Elizabethan England; his defence and fatherly protection of the baby is a powerful *human* moment in the play; it redeems Aaron from all the previous satanic evil. It is as if Shakespeare at the end of the play, having played up to popular prejudices about black people, suddenly decides to give the populace an alternative version, one in which blacks are proud, independent and human, and affected by paternal and filial emotions like everyone else. It is characteristic of Shakespeare that he takes on board a racial stereotype, he plays with it, feeding the prejudice of his audience, then withdraws the stereotype, undercuts it, demolishes it. In the *Merchant of Venice* for instance, Shylock is initially presented as a grasping Jew, after the fashion of Christopher Marlowe's Jew in the *Jew of Malta*, but at the height of the play, at the very beginning of Shylock's downfall he is given the most moving speech in the whole play, when he defends both his Jewishness and his desire for revenge:

> I am a Jew. Hath not a Jew eyes? Hath not a Jew hands, organs, dimensions, sense, affections, passions, fed with the same food, hurt with the same weapons, subject to the same diseases, healed by the same

means, warmed and cooled by the same winter and summer, as a
Christian is? If you prick us, do we not bleed? If you tickle us, do we not
laugh? If you poison us, do we not die? And if you wrong us, shall we
not revenge?

B. Shakespeare's *Othello, the Moor of Venice* (c. 1604)

Theatre audiences would have flocked to see Shakespeare's new
play, expecting to behold the antics of another black savage, a
Moor of Venice. Othello's first appearance on the stage would
have been one of the great moments in Elizabethan drama, for
instead of the wild and monstrous savage that was expected, there
is a commanding, imperious figure, totally calm and restrained
and in control of the situation. Muly Mahomet, Eleazor and
Aaron, when they make their first entrances, are full of long-
winded fury, but Othello is terse, self-controlled. Iago tells
Othello that Brabantio, Desdemona's father, has been abusing
him in such bitter terms that he Iago was barely able to restrain
himself from slaying Brabantio - Iago is hoping to get Othello
similarly worked up. Othello's response to this is terse, one-
lined: 'Tis better as it is.' Iago then advises Othello to hide from
Brabantio's wrath, but Othello dismisses this suggestion
immediately, and in proud, commanding fashion:

> Not I, I must be found
> My parts, my title and my perfect soul
> Shall manifest me rightly.

When Cassio meets him, he says, 'tis well I am found by you'.
Here then is a strong, upright, self-assured black man - quite
unlike his predecessors Aaron, Eleazor and Muly Mahomet, who
at this point would either have been whining and contorting in
anger or distress, or else retreating to hide in some dark hole.
When Brabantio and Roderigo confront Othello and draw their
swords, Othello's deep voice rises commandingly over the
confusion, imposing stillness and order: 'Keep up your bright

swords, for the dew will rust them'. Othello, then, is the figure who stands for order and light. There is a powerful paradox here, for in this opening scene, taking place late at night, in the darkness and confusion, it is Othello, a *black* man, who is the symbol of light and order. The whole play reverses the conventions of darkness and light, for it is Othello the black man who is 'white' and Iago, the white man who is 'black'. As the Duke says of Othello, he is 'far more fair than black'. And it is Iago who is the devil figure, it is Iago who takes on the role of Aaron, Eleazor and Muly Mahomet in being the plotter and contriver of wicked schemes of destruction. This inversion of ideas about whiteness and blackness, goodness and evil, is a feature of the play. For instance, Othello, shocked by Desdemona's apparent infidelity calls her a '*fair* devil'; he broods on her betrayal: 'a fine woman, a *fair* woman ...'. He just cannot believe that the fairness or whiteness of her skin is not reflected in the fairness or purity of her morality. And, in the murder scene, as he leans over her, he cries, 'O thou *black* weed, why art so lovely fair', again unable to understand how whiteness and goodness are not identical.

Othello, at first a noble, rational, self-assured person, degenerates into a state of savagery. 'I'll tear her all to pieces', he cries out in the extremity of passion, 'I will chop her into mess', 'O blood, Iago, blood'. These cannibalistic images mean that Othello has taken on the features of Aaron, Eleazor and Muly Mahomet. He begins to rant and froth, losing all rationality, this process of intellectual breakdown signalled in the disintegration of his language which, starting off as an eloquent and poetic speech at the beginning of the play, ends up as a series of staccato outbursts: 'Pish! Noses, ears and lips. Is it possible? Confess? Handkerchief? O devil!', he cries out in his madness. Othello also reverts to heathen superstition - he tells Desdemona of the magical power of the handkerchief, spun by some Egyptian witch, and that once the handkerchief is lost, their relationship is doomed and the charm broken. This degeneration into paganism at the end of the play fulfils Brabantio's earlier accusation that Othello has used primitive, African magic to charm and seduce Desdemona, a charge which Othello had vigorously denied. Now at the end of the play he is shown as a believer in pagan mysteries. In other words, Othello has *become* a 'black', taking on all the attributes of the mythical blacks listed in the travel books. Even his physical appearance has become ugly and stereotypical: as he leans over Desdemona to kill her, his eyes roll in the way that Africans in English demonology have rolling eyes. 'And yet I fear you for you are fatal then / when your eyes roll so', Desdemona cries out in fear. In *Titus Andronicus* Aaron had started off as a savage, degenerate creature, and ended up as a humane person; Shakespeare had started with the myth but ended with the reality of blacks. In *Othello,* this process is reversed. Othello begins as a noble, rational human being, and ends up as a raving, bloodthirsty animal - in other words, Othello grows into the myth, he becomes the mythical African, so that at the end Emelia calls him a 'black Devil'. Shakespeare shows how the mythical African is the creation of the white man and the white mind, for it is Iago who transforms Othello into a 'black ' man, it is Iago who *creates* the monster. 'Blacks' are made by whites. Othello himself begins to believe in his 'blackness' - at the crux of the play he breaks down and begins to accept his inferiority as a human being: 'Haply for I am black' he whimpers. Desdemona too is a victim of mythmaking. How much is her love of Othello based on intimate understanding of him as a person, and how much on her attraction to exotica? Women were avid readers of travel books. In her attraction to Othello's stories about exotic landscape, with its strange forms of life ('cannibals' and 'anthropophagi'), and in her sympathy for his travails, is Desdemona not an exemplary 'travel book fan'?

C. Shakespeare's *The Tempest* (c. 1611)

The Tempest is a study in power, the exercise of power and the liberation from the stranglehold of power - these dark and profound issues set in a deceptively naive environment of magic, masque and enchantment. Jan Kott, the Polish critic, in his book *Shakespeare our Contemporary*, disputes the traditional reception of the play as an idyllic dream-play: 'Commentators on *The Tempest* find on this island the idyllic atmosphere of Arcadia. No doubt they interpret the play only through bad theatre performances; those with a ballet-dancer and a translucent screen. They see fairy-tale and ballet all the time.' Jan Kott prefers to see the dream element in *The Tempest* as tending more to nightmare, with the features of Gothic fantasy:

> On Prospero's island, Shakespeare's history of the world is played out, in an abbreviated form. It consists of a struggle for power, murder, revolt and violence. Prospero's island has nothing in common with the happy isles of Renaissance utopias. It rather reminds us of the islands in the world of the late Gothic. Such worlds were painted by one of the greatest visionaries among painters, precursor of the Baroque and Surrealism, the mad Hieronymus Bosch. The islands rise out of a grey sea. They are brown or yellow. They take the form of a cone, reminding one of a volcano, with a flat top. On such hills, tiny human figures swarm and writhe like ants. The scenes depict the seven deadly sins and the human passions, above all lechery and murder, drunkenness and gluttony. As well as people there are demons with beautiful, slender, angelic female bodies and toads' or dogs' heads. These islands are gardens of torment, scenes of the world's cruel tortures. In that world Shakespeare was a witness.

The theme of power is introduced at the very beginning of the play. In the chaos and cruelty of the storm, men degenerate into terror and weakness. Before the power of Nature, all mankind is powerless; as the mariner says, 'What cares these roarers for the name of King!' In the following scene, we are told of the effects of *political* power - we hear Prospero's story of murder and betrayal, the story of his brother Antonio's greed for power and his usurpation of the Dukedom of Milan. The next scene continues the exploration of power: we see Ariel utterly submissive to the will of Prospero. Ariel's first words acknowledge his powerlessness, his subservience:

> All hail, great master! grave sir, hail! I come
> To answer thy best pleasure; be it to fly,
> To swim, to dive into the fire, to ride
> On the curlèd clouds, to thy strong bidding task
> Ariel and all his quality.

Later in the same scene Ariel rebels against Prospero's dictates. We see Ariel attempting to negotiate his freedom from Prospero's power:

> *Ariel*   Is there more toil? Since thou dost give me pains,
> Let me remember ᵗhee what thou hast promised,
> Which is not yet performed me.
> *Prospero* How now? moody? What is it thou canst demand?
> *Ariel*   My liberty.
> *Prospero* Before the time be out? no more!
> *Ariel*   I prithee, remember I have done thee worthy service;
> Told thee no lies, made thee no mistakings, served
> Without grudge or grumblings: thou didst promise
> To bate me a full year.

Such tension between master and slave is surcharged upon Caliban's first entrance. The exchange between Prospero and Caliban is a power struggle. Caliban, bearing a log of wood, is an image of slavery. He is repeatedly described as a slave - 'Thou poisonous slave', 'abhorred slave', 'So slave, hence!', 'What, ho! Slave! Caliban!'. He in turn accuses Prospero of fraudulent kingship, curses him for usurping the island in the same way that Antonio had usurped Prospero's dukedom:

> This island's mine, by Sycorax my mother,
> Which thou takest from me. When thou camst first,
> Thou strok'dst me, and made much of me; wouldst give me
> Water with berries in't, and teach me how
> To name the bigger light, and how the less,
> That burn by day and night: and then I loved thee
> And show'd thee all the qualities of the isle,
> The fresh springs, brine-pits, barren place and fertile:
> Cursèd be I that did so! All the charms
> Of Sycorax, toads, beetles, bats, light on you!
> For I am all the subjects that you have,
> Which first was mine own king; and here you sty me
> In this hard rock, whiles you do keep from me
> The rest of the island.

In the following scenes other acts of murder or grasping for power are enacted or plotted - we see Antonio urging Sebastian to murder his sleeping brother Alonso, King of Naples, and so inherit the throne of Naples. Antonio persuades him of the advantage of murder and confesses that he himself had readily supplanted his brother Prospero -

> And look how well my garments sit upon me;
> Much feater than before: my brother's servants
> Were then my fellows; now they are my men.

Antonio in other words has moved from being relatively powerless to being the ruler of men, and murder justifies the end. Asked by Sebastian whether he feels any prick of conscience he declares, 'I feel not this deity in my bosom'. Such exploration of the dark psychology of the lust for power dominates the play and is reflected even in the comic sub-plot. Stephano and Trinculo, the two clowns, get Caliban, whom they call their 'servant-monster' drunk, and Caliban swears servitude to them - 'How does thy honour? Let me lick thy shoe!', he says, and promises them ownership of the island: 'Thou shall be lord of it and I'll serve thee'. Stephano and Trinculo then go off looking for Prospero, to kill him. They discover Prospero's wardrobe, they put on his garments and play at being kings of the island, in an episode that is a parody of the play's theme of the usurpation of power. It is against this background of grasping human passions that Shakespeare proposes an alternative vision of human life. The alternative vision resides in Gonzalo's utterance on the commonwealth, a vision of democracy and communism:

> No name of magistrate,
> Letters should not be known; riches, poverty,
> And use of service, none: contract, succession,
> Bourn, bound of land, corn, or wine, or oil;
> No occupation: all men idle, all;
> All women too, but innocent and pure,
> No sovereignty; -
> ...
> All things in common nature should produce
> Without sweat or endeavour: treason, felony,
> Sword, pike, knife, gun or need of any engine
> Would I not have; but nature should bring forth
> Of it own kind, all foison, all abundance,
> To feed my innocent people.

The alternative vision of human possibilities resides too in the relationship between Ferdinand and Miranda. Ferdinand is enslaved by Prospero, as Caliban and Ariel are, but finds freedom in his love for Miranda:

> Might I but through my prison once a day
> Behold this maid: all corners else of the earth
> Let liberty make use of; space enough
> Have I in such a prison;

Later on, Ferdinand, bearing a log on his back like a slave, confesses his love for Miranda using the language of power and slavery that dominates the play -

> I am in my condition
> A prince, Miranda; I do think, a king;
> I would, not so! - and would no more endure
> This wooden slavery than to suffer
> The flesh-fly blow my mouth.
> Hear my soul speak:
> The very instant that I saw you, did
> My heart fly to your service; there resides,
> To make me slave to it; and for your sake
> Am I this patient log-man.

Miranda responds by saying that she will be the one to serve him - 'I will be your servant / whether you will or no'. The play on the concepts of power, slavery, rulership and bondage continues:

> *Ferdinand*: My mistress, dearest,
>   And I thus humble ever
> *Miranda*: My husband then?
> *Ferdinand*: Ay, with a heart as willing
>   As bondage e'er of freedom

What Shakespeare is doing is introducing into the play new concepts about power, rulership and servitude. The love between Ferdinand and Miranda redefines the power relationship. *Romantic slavery* - enslavement to love - stands in positive contrast to the *Political slavery* that characterizes the relationship between Prospero, Sebastian, Alonso and Antonio.

There is in the play a third kind of slavery, which has to do with European conquest and colonization, and which is suggested in the relationship between Prospero and Caliban. For

Caliban is the native colonized and dispossessed by the European. The play itself was, it is said, inspired by an incident involving Empire - in 1609, a year or two before *The Tempest* was written, a fleet of English ships sent out to Virginia was caught up in a storm, and one vessel was driven ashore on the Bermudas. The crew of this vessel remained on one of the Bermudan islands for several months, until they could build a new ship to take them to Virginia. News of the disaster spread through England, and in 1610, an account of the sojourn on Bermuda was published in the form of a tract entitled *A Discovery of the Bermudas, otherwise called the Isle of Devils,* full of curious tales of strange noises, spirits, devils and so on. The atmosphere of *The Tempest* and the reference to the 'still-vexed Bermoothes' (I, 2, 229) tend to confirm the view that the play was inspired by these New World events. There are several references to the New World in the play, to anthropophagi, the mythical African hybrid humans who had heads in their chests (III, 3, 50), to American Indians being put on display in London (II, 2, 20), and so on. Gonzalo's speech on the commonwealth referred to earlier is borrowed directly from Montaigne's essay 'Of the Cannibals', an essay which argued that the life of South American Indians showed that mankind was capable of living peacefully, happily and humanely without the constraint of law or the institution of private property. There was, at the time largely through the influence of travel books, great curiosity about the lifestyle and mores of non-European societies, curiosity out of which mythic structures evolved: put simply, the Carib or American Indian was conceived either as a Noble Savage or else as a degenerate species of humanity. Caliban is an ambiguous character, his nature is stretched over both mythic poles. On the one hand, he is a naive or unsophisticated creature, easily made drunk and corrupted by the whites (the episode with the alcohol is terribly prophetic of the way Europeans were to corrupt the nature of the natives, and get them to sign over their lands under the influence of whisky). Caliban is a 'noble savage' too in his immediate and sensuous response to nature. He has an innate feeling for natural beauty:

Be not afeard; the isle is full of noises
Sounds and sweet airs, that give delight and hurt not.
Sometimes a thousand twanging instruments
Will hum about mine ears, and sometime voices
That, if I had wak'd after long sleep,
Will make me sleep again: and then, in dreaming,
The clouds methought would open, and show riches
Ready to drop upon me; that when I wak'd
I cried to dream again.

On the other hand he is endowed with some of the chief characteristics of the degenerate alien - he is physically ugly, he is half-monster, half-fish, half-man; he is sexually corrupt, weaving fantasies of raping the young Miranda. Shakespeare thus creates a Caliban who is ambiguous, but whose ambiguity reflects the contradictory philosophic formulations of Europeans about non-European peoples. It is characteristic of Shakespeare that he should present and explore rather than resolve the contradictions - Othello and Aaron are similarly complex and contradictory, being both savage *and* noble; perpetrators of bloodshed *and* victims of white deceit and white manipulation.

D. Daniel Defoe's *Robinson Crusoe* (1719)

'Industry' was a key term in the eighteenth century, frequently evoked by pamphleteers and poets alike in their exhortations to the nation. In his poem *The Castle of Indolence*, James Thomson urges people to be sobre and diligent:

Toil and be glad! Let Industry inspire
Into your quickened limbs her buoyant breath!
Better the toiling swain, oh happier far!
Perhaps the happiest of the sons of men!
Who vigorous plies the plough, the team, or car,
Who houghs the field, or ditches in the glen,
Delves in his garden, or secures his pen:

> The tooth of avarice poisons not his peace;
> He tosses not in sloth's abhorred den.

John Dyer, in his poem *The Fleece,* urges the workers to be cheerful in their tasks - 'Blithe over your toil with wonted song proceed'. Industry, Dyer claimed, 'lifts the swain / And the straw cottage to a palace turns', a sentiment that echoes Thomson's view that through industry 'the poor man's lot with milk and honey flows'.

Much of the literature on Industry was of course grotesque propaganda since the reality of peasant and labouring class life was a reality of poverty, food shortages and economic exploitation. There was opulence at one end of society, grinding poverty at the other:

> Here, whilst the proud their long-drawn pomps display
> There, the black gibbet glooms beside the way
> > (Oliver Goldsmith, 'Deserted Village')

Celebration of the work-ethic in the writings of Thomson, Dyer and others, was bound up with celebration of Britain's commercial strengths and achievements. Commerce is lauded as the catalyst of social, cultural and economic progress. As. T.K. Meier put it:

> Literary men of the seventeenth and eighteenth centuries, including Dryden, Pope, Steele, Thomson, most of the georgic poets, and a number of lesser dramatists, essayists, and poets did heap high praise upon both the concept of capitalistic business enterprise and upon businessmen who practiced it ... Commerce and industry had caught the literary imagination of the period and represented for a time at least, the progressive hope of the future.

But it was by the forced labour of Africans that much of the commercial development of Britain occurred. Blacks were crucial to the business of commerce and civilization . They were, in seventeenth and eighteenth century opinion, 'the strength and sinews of this western world' and 'the mainspring of the machine which sets every wheel in motion'.

Robinson Crusoe can be read as a celebration of the work-ethic. Comparison with previous 'island fictions' reveals how eighteenth-century the novel is. In Shakespeare's *The Tempest*

(c. 1611) for instance, the island is a place of magic and poetic strangeness. The dream island is the location for romance and reconciliation. Passions are becalmed, enmities healed. Later in the century we have another 'island fiction', a short novel by Henry Neville called *The Isle of Pines* (1688). The island in the novel is a place where, far from the scrutiny of Europe, Europeans can indulge in all kinds of sexual dreams and fantasies. The story is about a man who is shipwrecked upon an island, together with his master's daughter, his master's black servant woman, and two other women. The man soon takes the opportunity of making love to all of them, and they all bear him dozens of children, who then mate with each other, so that the whole island is soon populated. The shipwrecked islanders lose their European manners and modesty, and walk about stark naked. The island story is a male white dream or fantasy about indulging in sexual pleasures which *breach* the moral, religious and social codes of European society. By mating with his master's daughter for example, the man is breaching the class code; by mating with the black woman, he is breaching certain codes about good taste; by fathering several children by four mothers, he is breaching religious and moral codes about monogamy and fidelity.

By the time we come to *Robinson Crusoe*, the island fiction has nothing of the dream-magic of Shakespeare or the dream-fantasy of Neville. Defoe's dreams are totally dry. The island is a place where European skills can be applied to plant, cultivate and develop. Defoe's dreams are about the Protestant work-ethic.

The novel is an allegory on industry and development. Crusoe progresses from hunting (he goes out and shoots or traps animals) to farming (he plants maize), to manufacturing (he constructs a kiln to make pots and glassware). In this process of evolution from a primitive to a scientific condition, everything is submitted to economic judgement; the economic takes precedence over all aspects of human experience. Take the attitude to Nature - Crusoe's attitude to Nature is this: if it moves, eat it. There is nothing romantic or spiritual about Crusoe's response to nature. He is hard-headed, practical: trees exist to be cut down and hacked into boats, animals exist to be eaten or skinned, and the skins are commodities of trade. Or else animals exist to be domesticated and bred. It is always the economic that matters, not the spiritual. Everything is subject to calculation and accountancy: at one point, Crusoe, feeling sorry for himself in his loneliness, decides to weigh up his good experiences against his bad ones -

> I began to comfort my self as well as I could, and to set the good against the evil, that I might have something to distinguish my case from worse, and I stated it very impartially, like debtor and creditor, the comforts I enjoyed against the miseries I suffered, thus:

Evil	Good
I am cast upon a horrible desolate island, void of all hope of recovery.	But I am alive, and not drowned as all my ship's company was.
I am singled out and separated, as it were, from all the world to be miserable	But I am singled out too from all the ship's crew to be spared from death; and He that miraculously saved me from death, can deliver me from this condition.
I am divided from mankind, a solitaire, one banished from humane society.	But I am not starved and perishing on a barren place, affording no sustenance.
I have not clothes to cover me.	But I am in a hot climate, where if I had clothes I could hardly wear them

He sets one against the other as in a ledger book. This ledger book mentality is absurdly manifested when Crusoe saves Friday by killing the Indian savages out to eat him. After the combat, Crusoe, true to form, counts the dead -

> 3 killed at our first shot from the tree.
> 2 killed at the next shot.
> 2 killed by Friday in the boat.
> 2 killed by ditto, of those at first wounded.
> 1 killed by ditto, in the wood.
> 3 killed by the Spaniard.

4 killed, being found dropped here and there of their wounds, or
   killed by Friday in his chase of them.
4 escaped in the boat, whereof one wounded if not dead.

21 in all.

All this may seem rather charming in its oddity and eccentricity,
but when Crusoe's ledger book philosophy is applied to blacks it
is deeply dangerous. Crusoe for instance sells Xury, the black boy
who had helped him escape from slavery, even though Xury was
his devoted friend. Later, when Crusoe needs help in working his
plantation, he misses not having Xury around - 'I wanted help,
and now I found more than before, I had done wrong in parting
with my boy Xury'. But by 'wrong', Crusoe does not mean moral
wrong, but economic mistake. 'Wrong' is defined economically,
not morally. Crusoe has no moral qualms about buying black
slaves, and breeding them like goats, to work on his Brazilian
plantation. What matters is the productiveness and profitability
of the plantation, not the moral aspect of slavery. Indeed his
shipwreck resulted from a slaving voyage to Guinea - he leaves
his plantation to trade in slaves, so as to increase his revenue.
Looking back on this move Crusoe calls it 'evil', but by 'evil' he
does not mean the moral evil of enslaving blacks but the 'evil' of
economic miscalculation - leaving his prosperous plantation to
gamble on making more money by slave merchandise. Again, it
is the ledger book philosophy in which ethics give way to
economics.

As to the relationship between Crusoe and Friday, it is a
paradigm of the master-slave relationship, in which the slave is
depicted as being grateful to his master for saving his life. One of
the excuses for slavery was that it was benevolent. John Dunton
argued that the Slave Trade saved Africans from the bloody
tyranny of their own countrymen, and saved them from being
eaten by their fellow cannibals. Crusoe saving Friday is a
re-enactment of the myth of salvation. Friday is devoted, he is glad
to learn, glad to serve and happy in his servitude. He is dazzled by
the skills and the science of the white man. Crusoe also saves his

soul by turning him into a Protestant, and this missionary
benevolence justifies the master-slave relationship.

E. Joseph Conrad's *Heart of Darkness* (1902)

Conrad's *Heart of Darkness* offers a powerful denunciation of the
horrors of Imperialism in its depiction of the cruelty of
Europeans and the decimation of native Africans. In the greed for
ivory and quick profit, life is smashed up and squandered. The
Congo has become 'a merry dance of death and trade in an
overheated catacomb'. The Africans are literally worked to the
bone, reduced to utter weariness, almost apathy to pain, then put
out to die:

> Black shapes crouched, lay, sat between the trees leaning against the
> trunks, clinging to the earth, half-coming out, half-effaced within the
> dim light, in all the attitudes of pain, abandonment and despair. They
> were dying slowly - it was very clear. They were not enemies, they were
> not criminals, they were nothing earthly now - nothing but black
> shadows of disease and starvation lying confusedly in the greenish
> gloom. Brought from all the recesses of the coast in all the legality of
> time contracts, lost in uncongenial surroundings, fed on unfamiliar
> food, they sickened, became inefficient, and were then allowed to crawl
> away and rest. These moribund shapes were free as air - and nearly as
> thin. I began to distinguish the gleam of the eyes under the trees. Then,
> glancing down, I saw a face near my hand. The black bones reclined at
> full length with one shoulder against the tree, and slowly the eyelids
> rose and the sunken eyes looked up at me, enormous and vacant, a kind
> of blind, white flicker in the depths of the orbs, which died out slowly.

In the scramble for wealth, the whites themselves become corrupt
and lunatic, the threshold of cruelty is lowered and there is
automatic resort to excessive, inhumane cruelty. Hence for
instance the over-reaction of one fat, sick white man being
carried through the bush, whose stretcher-bearers collapse under
the weight of his sixteen stones: 'I came upon the whole concern
wrecked in a bush - man, hammock, groans, blankets, horrors.

The heavy pole had skinned his poor nose. He was very anxious for me to kill somebody, but there wasn't the shadow of a carrier near.' A trifling accident is met with a lusty desire to execute the offenders. Such wanton behaviour reveals the way African life was considered to be *cheap* but also the extent to which white men in the Congo had divested themselves of moral restraints and civilized codes of behaviour. For white lives are also *cheapened*, not just in the metaphoric sense of the shedding of humane ideals, but in actuality: Marlow tells of the Belgian soldiers, some of whom would get swept away in the river in attempting to disembark, and drown: 'Whether they did or not, nobody seemed particularly to care. They were just flung out there, and on we went'. Others would die of tropical fever on board ships, but again, their deaths excited neither sorrow nor compassion. Such apathy, such *cheapening* of human life in the drive for the accumulation of wealth, creates an atmosphere of absurdity which is brilliantly exhibited in the story of Fresleven the Dane:

> It appears the Company had received news that one of their Captains had been killed in a scuffle with the natives. It was only months and months afterwards, when I made the attempt to recover what was left of the body, that I heard the original quarrel arose from a misunderstanding about some hens. Yes, two black hens. Fresleven - that was the fellow's name, a Dane - thought himself wronged somehow in the bargain, so he went ashore and started to hammer the chief of the village with a stick. Oh, it didn't surprise me in the least to hear this, and at the same time to be told that Fresleven was the gentlest, quietest creature that ever walked on two legs. No doubt he was; but he had been a couple of years already out there engaged in the noble cause, you know, and he probably felt the need at last of asserting his self-respect in some way. Therefore he whacked the old nigger mercilessly, while a big crowd of his people watched him, thunderstruck, till some man - I was told the chief's son - in desperation at hearing the old chap yell, made a tentative jab with a spear at the white man - and of course it went quite easy between the shoulderblades. Then the whole population cleared into the forest, expecting all kinds of calamities to happen, while, on the other hand, the steamer Fresleven commanded left also in a bad panic, in charge of the engineer, I believe. Afterwards nobody seemed to trouble much about Fresleven's remains, till I got out and stepped into his shoes. I couldn't let it rest though; but when an opportunity offered at last to meet my predecessor, the grass growing through his ribs was tall enough to hide his bones. They were all there.

Marlow's casual and distant tone of narration, his off-hand manner, his throw-away, almost flippant lines, convey perfectly the casual operation of murder in the bush. The novel teems with other examples of the grotesque and the absurd, the most striking being the episode in which a warship shells incomprehensibly into the bush at imagined natives - 'Pop, would go one of the six-inch guns; a small flame would dart and vanish, a little white smoke would disappear, a tiny projectile would give a feeble screech - and nothing happened. Nothing could happen. There was a touch of insanity in the proceedings, a sense of lugubrious drollery in the sight.' This comedy of disorder extends everywhere, permeates all European activities - from the setting up of dishevelled tin-can stations in the bush to the abandoning of broken machinery which lay rotting in the mud like the carcasses of dead animals. The dead African with a bullet-hole in his head whom Marlow stumbles upon in the bush connects up with the hole at the bottom of the bucket which prevents the putting out of the fire, and also with the vast artificial hole in the ground which Marlow one day discovers, the purpose of which puzzles him - 'I avoided a vast artificial hole somebody had been digging on the slope, the purpose of which I found it impossible to divine. It wasn't a quarry or a sandpit, anyhow. It was just a hole. It might have been connected with the philanthropic desire of giving the criminals something to do. I don't know.' These various holes symbolise the intellectual and human vacancy of the Belgian colonization of the Congo. They create or build nothing. Their attempts at order are shallow and idiotic. The Company's Chief Accountant in his starched white collar, white cuffs, white necktie, snowy trousers and varnished boots who extends his 'big white hand' to Marlow is a personified caricature of the light of civilization that was meant to justify European occupation of Africa. The neatness of the Chief Accountant's office, its ledger books and invoice registers in apple-pie order, is a perverse version of the order that was supposedly characteristic of European civilization, an order that in reality is callous and mean - the Chief Accountant for instance complains that the groans of a dying native distracts his computation 'When one has got to make correct entries', he complains, 'one comes to hate those savages - hate them to the death'.

There is, however, in the novel, in spite of all such savage and satiric indictments, an ambivalent attitude to Empire. What Marlow regrets and despises is not the ideal of Imperialism, but the corruption of that ideal. It is not the notion of Empire that is being attacked, but the reality of Empire as revealed in the Belgian Congo. Marlow, for instance, differentiates between *British* and *European* Empire-building. Looking upon a map of the world which is marked with all the colours of a rainbow, each colour signifying a colony belonging to a particular Western nation, he is scornful of European possessions. He speaks of 'smears of orange' and 'a purple patch to show where the jolly pioneers of progress drink the jolly lager-beer'. As to British possessions, 'There was a vast amount of red - good to see at any time, because one knows that some real work is done in there'. By 'real work' Marlow is referring to the building of roads, churches, libraries and the rest, by the British, as opposed to the disorderly plunder of European settlements. His chauvinism belongs to the spirit of these times, when Britain, Germany and the Western Nations were competing against each other for the title of 'Greatest Imperial Nation'. Marlow is indeed deeply romantic about the possibilities of British Imperialism. The Thames glittering in sunlight, in the opening chapter of the novel, is a symbol of the initial glamour of Empire. From that river had sailed forth British national heroes like Sir Francis Drake and Sir John Franklin on ships 'whose names are like jewels flashing in the night of time ... they all had gone forth out on that stream, bearing the sword, and often the torch, messengers of the might within the land, bearers of a spark from the sacred fire. What greatness had not floated on the ebb of that river into the mystery of an unknown earth! ... The dreams of men, the seed of commonwealths, the germs of empires'. In those early days the world seemed ripe for discovery, it was soaked in marvels and curiosities. There was the thrill of danger, the excitement and the romance of exotic encounters. As Marlow says, Africa was 'a blank space of delightful mystery - a white patch for a boy to dream gloriously over'. The idea of planting European civilization in the soil of Africa and the soul of its inhabitants had an air of missionary innocence to it. There was much work to be done, bush to be cleared, roads to be built, parliaments and churches to be set up, and so on. What Marlow laments is the loss of innocence, the loss and corruption of those early ideas which were gradually superseded by the lust for fortune in the form of ivory. The ivory is a dual symbol of both the ideal and the reality of Empire: its whiteness suggests the original Imperial dream of bringing light to the bush; at the same time, the ivory is the treasure that Europeans murder for. From being apostles of light, fired by missionary zeal, Europeans have become 'pilgrims' devoted to the worship of money. And with the civilizing ideal gone, colonization becomes a mere sordid business. As Marlow says, 'The conquest of the earth, which mostly means the taking it away from those who have a different complexion or slightly flatter noses than ourselves, is not a pretty thing when you look into it too much. What redeems it is the idea only. An idea at the back of it; not a sentimental pretence but an idea; and an unselfish belief in the idea - something you can set up, and bow down before, and offer a sacrifice to ...'

Which brings us to Kurtz whose personal history embodies the original dream, and the corruption of that dream. Kurtz started off with 'the idea, an unselfish belief in the idea - something you can set up and bow down before and offer a sacrifice to'; he ends up by setting himself up as a god before whom the natives bowed and made cannibalistic sacrifices. At the beginning he is a classical missionary figure, full of noble ideas about torch-bearing, about setting the bush alight with the concepts of European civilization. He believed then in a benevolent form of Imperialism; in his own words, 'By the simple exercise of our will we can exert a power for good practically unbounded'. His words, Marlow says, were 'burning, noble words'. Instead of the fulfilment of these burning ideals, Kurtz degenerates into an emaciated figure crawling on all fours. And the only burning that takes place in the novel is the fire which destroys the grass shed and which exposes the Europeans as ineffectual buffoons in their attempt to control it.

Kurtz's downfall - from his aspiration to benevolence to his outburst that all the natives should be exterminated - is attributed to the environment of Africa, and it is on this issue that Marlow confounds the previous attribution of corruption to European greed. Kurtz is an innocent tainted by the touch of Africa. He

107

cracks up in the environment of Africa because Africa is the location of overbearing and overwhelming satanic influences. In the Congo, the policemen and the butcher, in Marlow's own words, are absent - the policeman being representative of law and the butcher of order (the butcher brings commercial order to the process of appetite, as opposed to the anarchic slaughter and free-for-all cannibalism of the Congo). In such an environment, Kurtz is liberated from the codes of civilized behaviour - 'there was nothing on earth to prevent killing whom he jolly well pleased'. The spirit of Africa is monstrously sensual, it seduces him away from his original intellectual mission: 'the heavy mute spell of the wilderness seemed to draw him to its pitiless breast by the awakening of forgotten and brutal instincts, by the memory of gratified and monstrous passions. This alone, I was convinced, had driven him out to the edge of the forest, to the bush, towards the gleam of fires, the throb of drums, the drone of weird incantations; this alone had beguiled his unlawful soul beyond the bounds of permitted aspirations.' Kurtz, then, 'forgot himself amongst these people' - the scornful emphasis on 'these people' reveals a shift in Marlow's attitude to the African. In the early part of the novel there was compassion for the undeserved suffering of Africans, compassion based on the fact of their humanity. Marlow sees the Africans as human beings, persuades his white listeners of that humanity by familiarizing comparisons. For instance, explaining that some parts of the bush were totally abandoned because the natives were afraid of the coming of the Europeans to enslave them, Marlow says, "Well, if a lot of mysterious niggers armed with all kinds of fearful weapons suddenly took to travelling on the road from Deal and Gravesend, catching the yokels right and left to carry heavy loads for them, I fancy every farm and cottage thereabouts would get empty very soon'. Wondering at the tremor of far-off drums, Marlow suggests that the sound perhaps contained as profound a meaning as the sound of bells in a Christian country. A few pages before Marlow had come across a dying African who wore a piece of white string round his neck - 'He had tied a bit of white worsted round his neck - Why? Where did he get it? Was it a badge - an ornament - a charm - a propitiatory act? Was there any idea at all connected with it?' The implication here is that

Europeans, in their singular quest for ivory, wholly ignored African customs and rituals which, if enquired into, would reveal systems of logic and intellectuality indicative of their humanity. Marlow is almost calling for a serious anthropology of the Congo. But as the novel progresses Marlow begins to conceive of the African as the savage other, the primitive, the pre-human. The journey through the Congo becomes a journey through wholly unfamiliar, pre-human territory. 'We were wanderers on prehistoric earth, on an earth that wore an aspect of an unknown planet ... we were travelling in the night of first ages, of those ages that are gone, leaving hardly a sign - and no memories. The earth seemed unearthly ... and the men were - No, they were not inhuman. They howled and leaped and spun and made horrid faces; but what thrilled you was just the thought of their humanity - like yours - the thought of your remote kinship with this wild and passionate uproar.' From being people whose humanity is comparable to Europeans' on a civilized level, the Africans then became connected to them only as a revelation of their primitive capacities.

Kurtz's failure to sustain his original ambition of introducing civilization to the Congo is a testimony of the power of the forces of darkness over the forces of light and of the ultimate fragility, or vulnerability of European civilization before the swamping forces of savagery. At the beginning of the novel, Marlow had outlined this theme of the vulnerability of civilization. The Thames shimmering with light and the city of London humming with civilized activity are threatened by the coming of darkness: 'the sun sank low and from glowing white changed to a dull red without rays and without heat, as if about to go out suddenly, stricken to death by the touch of that gloom brooding over a crowd of men.' This descent into sinister darkness provokes from Marlow recollection of the dark pre-history of London, the great centre of Western civilization. 'And this also', Marlow said suddenly, 'has been one of the dark places of the earth'. The Knights of Light - the Sir Francis Drakes and Sir John Franklins - may have emerged from that river and city but only recently and in a minuscule flicker of civilization, a flicker that could so easily be extinguished by the vast enveloping presence of darkness. Marlow recounts the days of Roman Britain, when

Britain was a wilderness of death, when the towns feebly attempted to clear a moral space in the bush. 'Sand-banks, marshes, forests, savages - precious little to eat fit for a civilized man, nothing but Thames water to drink ... Here and there a military camp lost in a wilderness, like a needle in a bundle of hay - cold, fog, tempests, disease, exile and death - death skulking in the air, in the water, in the bush. They must have been dying like flies here'. London has evolved out of such savage squalor but could so easily revert back to it. The threat of barbarism is ever-present, it has to be guarded against constantly by the policeman and the butcher. The darkness is ever-present because it is embedded in the psychology of man, contained or repressed by a thin shell of moral idealism called 'Western Civilization'. Remove European man to Africa and he reverts to atavistic rituals and orgies of slaughter because his hold on civilized values is tenuous and only recently acquired. Kurtz for instance, succumbs to the bush, reduced by its dark whispers, 'because he was hollow to the core'. The skin of white rhetoric and rationality is stretched over a dark void.

Africa then is a place which unleashes forces of darkness and disorder in the human psyche. It is the testing-ground of the endurance or stability of white civilization and of the civilized white psyche. Conrad's purpose is to reveal the vulnerability of moral order, the weakness of the spirit of idealism before the overbearing power of original lust, of which Africa is a symbol. Kurtz degenerates from nobility of purpose to sadism, killing whom he pleases according to the unbridled thrust of his appetite, he becomes a megalomaniac, dreaming of kingship and world-domination. As Marlow says, 'he would have been a splendid leader of an extreme party'. And Africa is the catalyst for this process of human disintegration. Nor can the artefacts of European science and rationality take root in Africa - hence the rotting machinery, the broken and abandoned technology.

Conrad's concern with the heart of darkness that beats within humanity is of profound importance to our century. Certainly the explosion of barbarism in modern Europe between 1914 and 1945, validates Conrad's anxieties about the fragility of civilization. Kurtz as 'a potential leader of an extremist party' is the forerunner of the Fascist and Nazi rulers between the 1920s and 1940s who were swollen with ambitions of imposing order upon a complex and chaotic world, who built autobahns and made the trains run on time, but who ended up 'exterminating the brute' in gas-chambers and gravel pits. Conrad's anxieties were real but what is deeply fraudulent about the novel is its use of Africa as a symbol of darkness and a threat to Western civilization. For Africa has been an innocent witness to the havoc that white men have inflicted upon other white men in their World Wars. Africa did not instigate or participate in such organized mass murder; Africa did not unleash the forces of the subconscious.

F. John Buchan's *Prester John* (1910)

One can reduce Buchan's tale to its absurd essentials by saying it is a story about a Britisher and his dog who between them put down a great native uprising in Africa. It takes but one man and his dog to mow down the Africans and to keep them in their place. The man in fact started off as a boy but grew to manhood in Africa. Africa is the place where British youth is initiated into manhood, they have the opportunity to exercise their prowess, to marshall their courage, and to maintain a stiff upper lip in the face of extreme danger. The boy Davie who once played at being pirates and smugglers on the cliffs of Scotland later in life becomes embroiled in more real and manly adventures in Africa. From the humble and ordinary position of being an obscure student at Edinburgh University he becomes a widely-acclaimed hero in Africa. A great deal of the courage comes from being outnumbered - it's a case of a few white men against overwhelming odds. They exist at the edge of extinction - the sense of being swamped by overwhelming numbers, but the necessity of keeping the spirits up and sticking together in white solidarity, is a repetitive feature of the novel.

Davie's fear goes beyond that of being tortured and killed - it is the fear of not being man enough to rise to the occasion: 'I was horribly afraid of my impotence to play any manly part'. In a man's world impotence is not a sexual weakness but a weakness of patriotic virtue, a sense of letting the side down. The novel is very much about the ruggedness of a man's world - apart from the dumb black servant girl there are no women in it. The novel propagates public school hearty, manly virtues. The language teems with examples of public-school rhetoric about gamesmanship, evocative of the rugby field. 'He was an open enemy, playing a fair game', Davie says of Laputa. 'The first honours of the game had fallen to me' he says, in telling us of his clever entrance into Laputa's cave. When Laputa is cornered and about to be captured Davie again uses public-school language: 'His game was over and at our own leisure we could mop up the scattered concentrations'. Henriques, the Portuguese villain is described in public-school slang as 'a double-dyed traitor to his race'. Davie explodes into a hearty, public-school anger or petulance at one point: 'Very well, you yellow-faced devil, you will hear my answer. I would not take my freedom from you, though I were to be boiled alive. I know you for a traitor to the white man's cause, a dirty IDB swindler.' Henriques, who is a bit of a cad, has committed the ultimate public-school crime of cheating, of letting the side down by playing dirty with the opposition. And in all this, Davie laments the fact that his boyhood friend Tam could not be there to participate in 'the fun'. Africa then is the location for British public-school fun and manly games.

And yet, in spite of all the above, the novel is redeemed from an aggressive, hard-nosed imperialistic tone by two features - firstly, the sensitivity of Davie to his frailty. Again and again Davie confesses his physical weakness, his fear, his loneliness - human qualities which give the novel a human feel. Secondly, Davie's extraordinary sensitivity to the landscape of Africa. The land is not all bush and jungle-drums, but perceived with some delicacy, even love and admiration. In addition, landscape excites not only by its natural beauty, but because it reveals to Davie his own human frailty, his mortality. The crags and mountains over which he roams bruise his flesh, he is reduced to utter weariness and despair. The vast open spaces of Africa highlight his humanity and his insignificance:

> I knew now what starlight meant, for there was ample light to pick my way by. I steered by the Southern Cross, for I was aware that the Berg ran north and south, and with that constellation on my left hand I was bound to reach it sooner or later. The bush closed around me with its mysterious dull green shades, and trees, which in the daytime were thin scrub, now loomed like tall timber. It was very eerie moving, a tiny fragment of mortality, in that great wide silent wilderness, with the starry vault, like an impassive celestial audience, watching with many eyes. They cheered me, those stars. In my hurry and fear and passion they spoke of the old calm dignities of man.

Although *Prester John,* compared with other boys' adventure tales of the time, lacks a certain callousness and glorification of violence, it nevertheless depicts Africans in a negative light. The theme of adventure only works by presenting Africans as unfamiliar, mysterious creatures who share little with the whites. When Davie speaks of Africa as 'the theatre of so many strange doings' he is automatically distancing the blacks from the whites, denying a shared humanity. This bifurcation of black and white runs through the whole novel; it is revealed repeatedly in Davie's talk about 'our folk' and 'those natives'. Sentences like 'I thrilled with the thought that my *own* folk were at hand', or 'the fact that I was out of Kaffir country and in the land of my own folk was a kind of qualified liberty', or, worse still, 'behind me was heathendom and the black fever flats. In front were the cool mountains and bright streams and the guns of my own folk', abound. The cumulative effect is to create a stark, unbridgeable divide between blacks and whites, to give a sense that nothing can be shared. Blunt black-and-white choices have to be made. Either blacks have power, or else whites have power - there can be no equality, only rule and subjection, superiority and sub-servience.

Davie's benevolent imperialist philosophy is expressed at the end of the novel, when he summarizes his experience of Africa:

> Yet it was an experience for which I shall ever be grateful, for it turned me from a rash boy into a serious man. I knew then the meaning of the white man's duty. He has to take all risks, reckoning nothing of his life or his fortunes, and well content to find his reward in the fulfilment of

his task. That is the difference between white and black, the gift of responsibility, the power of being in a little way a king; and so long as we know this and practise it, we will rule not in Africa alone but wherever there are dark men who live only for the day and their own bellies.

In the end, the bush is turned into an orderly town, with a tobacco factory, an irrigation dam, industrial workshops, public-baths and a reading room. 'We have cleaned up the kraals', Wardlaw announces, 'and the chiefs are members of our county council'. This urban mediocrity, this banality of organization, is what Davie's grand words about civilizing the savage boils down to. It is the triumph of the British middle-class shopkeeper spirit over the supposed backwardness of Africa. The novel is almost parodying its own imperialistic philosophy. Indeed, parody is ever-present, specially in the silly passages dealing with Colin, the dog. The killing of Colin is described as a dastardly crime, the height of inhumanity. Davie resolves to kill Henriques, 'the yellow devil who has murdered my dog and my friends' - note the priority of the dog over the friends, as if the dog's life was more important. The dog is indispensable in the grand negotiations between Davie and Laputa for the recovery of the symbolic necklace. Chapter 16 ends on this sombre, statesmanlike and honourable note:

> 'Swear to me in turn,' I said, 'that you will give me my life if I restore the jewels.'
> He swore, kissing the book like a witness in a police-court. I had forgotten that the man called himself a Christian.
> 'One thing more I ask,' I said. 'I want my dog decently buried'.
> 'That has been already done,' was the reply. 'He was a brave animal, and my people honour bravery.'

Chapter 22 ends with the erection of a monument for the dog who is accorded the highest place in the canine canon of heroes:

> I found a mason in the Iron Kranz village, and from the excellent red stone of the neighbourhood was hewn a square slab with an inscription. It ran thus: 'Here lies buried the dog Colin, who was killed in defending D. Crawfurd, his master. To him it was mainly due that the Kaffir Rising failed.' I leave those who have read my tale to see the justice of the words.

Another example of the undermining of imperialist certainties lies in the representation of Laputa, the black leader. He is a powerful human being, possessed of a superior intellect and superior oratory. Davie is constantly stilled by his superior eloquence and dignity, and sometimes reduced into an insignificant boy. Take for example this extraordinary debate between the coloniser and the colonised:

He told me the story of the Machudi war, which I knew already, but he told it as a sage. There had been a stratagem by which one of the Boer leaders - a Grobelaar, I think - got some of his men into the enemy's camp by hiding them in a captured forage-wagon.

'Like the Trojan horse,' I said involuntarily.

'Yes,' said my companion, 'the same old device,' and to my amazement he quoted some lines of Virgil.

'Do you understand Latin?' he asked.

I told him that I had some slight knowledge of the tongue, acquired at the university of Edinburgh. Laputa nodded. He mentioned the name of a professor there, and commented on his scholarship.

'Oh man!' I cried, 'what in God's name are you doing in this business? You that are educated and have seen the world, what makes you try to put the clock back? You want to wipe out the civilization of a thousand years, and turn us all into savages. It's the more shame to you when you know better.'

'You misunderstand me,' he said quietly. 'It is because I have sucked civilization dry that I know the bitterness of the fruit. I want a simpler and better world, and I want that world for my own people. I am a Christian, and will you tell me that your civilization pays much attention to Christ? You call yourself a patriot? Will you not give me leave to be a patriot in turn?'

'If you are a Christian, what sort of Christianity is it to deluge the land with blood?'

'The best,' he said. 'The house must be swept and garnished before the man of the house can dwell in it. You have read history. Such a purging has descended on the Church at many times, and the world has awakened to a new hope. It is the same in all religions. The temples grow tawdry and foul and must be cleansed, and, let me remind you, the cleanser has always come out of the desert.'

I had no answer, being too weak and forlorn to think. But I fastened on his patriotic plea.

'Where are the patriots in your following? They are all red Kaffirs crying for blood and plunder. Supposing you were Oliver Cromwell you could make nothing out of such a crew.'

'They are my people,' he said simply.

Here, Davie's ignorance is exposed by contrast with the erudition of Laputa. Laputa's self-control forces Davie to hysterical outbursts which in turn produce only calmness and certainty in Laputa. Davie's loose allusion to Oliver Cromwell in the end reveals a loss of intellectual control, a loss of argument. Such sympathetic exposure to the black viewpoint is rare in boys' stories of the period. Although Laputa dies, and his rebellion dissipates, he nevertheless retains enormous stature within the story. He is its most memorable and persuasive character.

Prester John, then, is contradictory in its attitude to blacks and to Empire. Buchan is deliberate in his undermining of imperialism, and at the same time making Davie win. Buchan has inherited the boys' adventure story genre, with its aggressive arrogant and racist features, but he has subverted the genre by parody, and by presenting Davie as weak before the landscape of Africa and the character of Laputa. In 1910 that was as far as Buchan could go. Although Laputa is represented as a noble individual, the rest of the Africans are still the 'savage other'. They are described as 'burly savages', 'bloodthirsty savages' and 'brutes'. Indeed, Laputa is only accorded a status equivalent to the European because he was educated in Europe. Even his appearance is not 'negroid' - 'He had none of the squat and preposterous Negro lineaments'. Humanity then is only accorded to the African if he resembles the European in thinking and physical appearance. If he lacks these features the African is relegated to the status of the 'savage other'.

Section 3: Black British Literature

A. Early Writers: Equiano's *The Interesting Narrative* (1789; Reprinted in 1969 by Heinemann)

> The slaves lie in two rows, one above the other, like books upon a shelf. I have known them so close that the shelf could not, easily, contain one more.
>
> (John Newton: *Thoughts upon the African Slave Trade*, 1788, p. 33- 4)

The use of a library image to describe the interior of a slave-ship reveals the essential contradiction of the slave trade, namely that its barbarities were conducted by men of learning and civilization. James Houstoun, writing in 1724, described the Directors of the Royal African Company as 'a society of the politest gentlemen in the known world'. The library image also serves to put black literary achievement in its proper context: in the eighteenth century, blacks progressed from being packed like books aboard the slave-ship to being authors of books, moving from a situation of human squalor and passivity to one of creativity.

For black people, to write at all was a matter of achievement, given their status as slaves and outcasts in British society, and the poverty and illiteracy that was their lot. In eighteenth century Britain, lower-class whites were denied access to education and when philanthropists like Thomas Coram attempted to set up charity schools for poor white children, they were constantly subjected to criticism from the middle and upper classes. Such education was seen as posing a threat to the social order; there was a fear that the system of social subordination would dissolve if the lower classes acquired skills and education and began to entertain ideas above their station. The Sunday schools and charity schools set up by the Churches were basically designed to train the lower classes in the habits of industry and piety, sobriety and diligence - in other words to sustain the work ethic - and not to train the lower classes to question the *status quo* or to think for themselves. The situation of blacks, a group lower on the social scale than poor whites, would have been worse. Access to education would have been denied them so as to keep them in their place, just as access to skills were denied them to maintain their dependence: in 1731, the Lord Mayor issued a Proclamation banning the apprenticeship of black people -

> It is ordered by this Court that for the future no Negroes or other blacks be suffered to be bound Apprentices at any of the Companies of this City to any Freeman thereof; and that copies of this Order be printed and sent to the Masters and Wardens of the several Companies of this City, who are required to see the same at all times duly observed.

Ignatius Sancho, the black writer, stated in 1776 that 'I was placed in a family who judged ignorance the best and only security for obedience. A little reading and writing I got by unwearied application'. By 'unwearied application' Sancho would have meant stealthily stealing books from his master's library and working on them in his spare time, when no one was looking. He would have been taught some English, so as to make him a better servant, so that he could understand orders and perform tasks, but Sancho and his fellow blacks would have supplemented this basic instruction by stealthy reading. The danger that educated and literate blacks posed to the social system which held them in bondage is vividly illustrated by Equiano. Equiano, having been a slave in England from the age of 12, was taught to read and was sent to school through the kindness of two ladies who were relatives of his owner. Then without warning, the owners sold Equiano to a ship captain, Captain James Doran, who was about to set sail for the West Indies. Equiano protested against this transaction and attempted to resist being deported from the country:

> But just as we had got a little below Gravesend, we came alongside of a ship which was going away the next tide for the West Indies; her name was the *Charming Sally*, Captain James Doran, and my master went on

board and agreed with him for me, and in a little time I was sent for into the cabin. When I came there Captain Doran asked me if I knew him; I answered that I did not; 'Then,' said he, 'you are now my slave'. I told him my master could not sell me to him, nor to anyone else. 'Why,' said he, 'did not your master buy you?' I confessed he did. 'But I have served him,' said I, 'many years, and he has taken all my wages and prize-money, for I only got one sixpence during the war; besides this I have been baptized, and by the laws of the land no man has a right to sell me.' And I added that I had heard a lawyer and others at different times tell my master so. They both then said that those people who told me so were not my friends, but I replied, 'It was very extraordinary that other people did not know the law as well as they.' Upon this Captain Doran said I talked too much English, and if I did not behave myself well and be quiet he had a method on board to make me. I was too well convinced of his power over me to doubt what he said, and my former sufferings in the slave-ship presenting themselves to my mind, the recollection of them made me shudder.

Here we have a literate and informed black arguing for his civil rights. His logic and his command of English is so startling to the slave-owner that he is threatened with punishment if he does not shut up. Blacks were shut up in a variety of ways. Equiano tells of how, as a boy-slave in Virginia, he worked for a plantation owner whose black cook prepared the owner's food with an iron muzzle locked over her mouth to prevent her eating any of it:

While I was in this plantation the gentleman to whom I suppose the estate belonged being unwell, I was one day sent for to his dwelling house to fan him; when I came into the room where he was I was very much affrighted at some things I saw, and the more so as I had seen a black woman slave as I came through the house who was cooking the dinner, and the poor creature was cruelly loaded with various kinds of iron machines; she had one particularly on her head which locked her mouth so fast that she could scarcely speak, and could not eat nor drink. I was much astonished and shocked at this contrivance, which I afterwards learned was called the iron muzzle.

The muzzling of blacks was therefore physical and intellectual - in the case of the black cook it was an attempt to prevent her eating food, in the case of the black writer it was an attempt to prevent him writing at all.

The crucial reason, then, why education was denied blacks was to maintain their powerlessness, to maintain their condition of servility and dependency. Moreover the whole justification for the slave trade lay in the definition of blacks as sub-humans, devoid of intellectual faculties and incapable of betterment. Otherwise how could the white man *morally* justify the enslavement of his fellow human beings? It was repeatedly asserted by the most eminent white intellectuals of the day that blacks were not quite human beings, since they lacked the necessary intellectual apparatus which defines human beings. Lord Chesterfield for instance, a leading man of letters, and self-styled guardian of civilized values, declared that Africans were 'the most *ignorant* and unpolished people in the world, little better than lions, tigers, leopards and other wild beasts which that country produces in great numbers'. From this definition of blacks as sub-humans, Chesterfield goes on to argue that it was thus *morally* acceptable 'to buy a great many of them to sell again to advantage in the West Indies'. Here we have a clear and incontrovertible instance of the supposed stupidity of blacks being used as a justification for their enslavement. Their supposed stupidity also justified their cruel usage and the physical punishments meted out to them to make them work - it was no more cruel than beating an ass, because, it was argued, blacks were the equivalent of asses. William Knox, for instance, writing in 1768, deemed blacks to be 'the complete definition of indolent stupidity ... the stupid obstinacy of the Negroes may indeed make it always necessary to subject them to severe discipline from their masters ... It is no wonder that they are treated like brute beasts ... if they are incapable of feeling mentally, they will the more frequently be made to feel in their flesh'. When black people like Francis Williams read mathematics at Cambridge and showed themselves capable of writing *Latin* odes - that is, showed themselves capable of living up to English definitions of education - they were dismissed as freak blacks, accidents of nature, the exceptions that proved the rule.Edward Long called Francis Williams 'a rare phenomenon' implying that his literary talents were one-off. David Hume, the philosopher, took a similar line to Edward Long, arguing that blacks were intellectually inferior to whites, and that Francis Williams' Latin poetry was a paltry business:

> I am apt to suspect the negroes, and in general all other species of men (for there are four or five different kinds) to be naturally inferior to the whites. There never was a civilized nation of any other complexion than white, nor even any individual eminent either in action or speculation. No ingenious manufacture amongst them, no arts, no sciences. On the other hand, the most rude and barbarous of the white, much as the ancient Germans, the present Tartars, have still something eminent about them, in their valour, form of government, or some other particular. Such a uniform and constant difference could not happen, in so many countries and ages, if nature had not made an original distinction betwixt these breeds of men. Not to mention our colonies, there are Negro slaves disposed all over Europe, of which none ever discovered any symptoms of ingenuity, though low people will start up amongst us [whites] and distinguish themselves in every profession. In Jamaica indeed they talk of one negro as a man of parts and learning [Francis Williams], but 'tis likely he is admired for very slender accomplishments, like a parrot who speaks a few words plainly.

Others hostile to blacks attacked the evidence of black learning, exemplified in black writing, on grounds of merit or quality. Thus Ignatius Sancho's literary letters were dismissed as 'little more than commonplace effusions' and Phyllis Wheatley's poems were 'below the dignity of criticism'. In other words, the writings of Sancho and Wheatley were judged to be aesthetically inferior and mediocre compared with good European literature. This aesthetic critique of black writing has to be tackled head on, since it is the most common trick that white literary scholars employ to denigrate black writing. Phyllis Wheatley's poems were written in the poetic idiom of the eighteenth century - an artificial, rhetorical idiom - and she compares well with English poets of the period of the order of, say, Matthew Prior, or Edward Young, or James Grainger (minor but typical English poets of the century). *No-one* compares with John Dryden or Alexander Pope, so it is futile and ignorant to judge black poetry against their poetic genius. As to working-class poetry, the eighteenth century only threw up a few writers like Mary Collier, formerly a washerwoman, and Stephen Duck, a farm hand. Phyllis Wheatley's poems stand up well compared with the verse of Mary Collier and Stephen Duck, in terms of the felicity of diction, phrasing, imagery and rhythm. When one takes into account that Phyllis Wheatley was a slave-woman, then these purely aesthetic comparisons become absurd. The literature has to be judged not narrowly by criteria of form, but also by consideration of its social context and repercussions.

A final trick to denigrate black writing was to deny that it was written by blacks at all. Phyllis Wheatley, to avoid any allegation that her poems were 'ghosted' had a document of authenticity inserted into her volume of poetry, signed by respectable men of learning, including five Doctors of Divinity. 'We, whose names are underwritten, do assure the world, that the poems specified in the following pages were (as we verily believe) written by Phyllis, a young African girl, who was but a few years since, brought an uncultivated barbarian from Africa, and has ever since been, as now is, under the disadvantage of serving as a slave in a Family in this town. She has been examined by some of the best judges, as is thought qualified to write them'. This certificate is indicative of a historical experience of black people. When they were captured on the West African coast and sold to slave merchants, bills of sale were issued to those slave-owners; when they were unloaded in the West Indies and auctioned, again certificates of sale were made out to the purchasers and owner's initials branded their bodies. When blacks, like Equiano, saved up their pennies over the years and bought their own freedom, a certificate of freedom was issued which was their most precious possession, carried about their body wherever they went as protection against future enslavement; even black writers needed a certificate of authenticity before they could be recognised. This experience of certification has endured into our present day. With the passing of Immigration and Nationality laws and with the institution of a variety of rules and tests, black people in Britain today have their papers as their most precious possessions - a passport, a National Health Card, a National Insurance Card. So when Phyllis Wheatley was properly certified she was undergoing a process fundamental to blacks. Equiano had a similar problem - his African origins were disputed in the wake of the enormous success of his book - two newspapers in 1792, *The Star* and *The Oracle* alleged that Equiano was not African at all but a native of Santa Cruz, a Danish island in the Caribbean. The *Monthly Review* doubted Equiano's authorship, arguing that 'it is not improbable that some *English* writer assisted him in the compilation, or at least the correction of his book, for it is sufficiently well written'.

It was essential for some people to deny the literary merit and even the authorship of black writing, for not to do so would be to expose the basic philosophical pillar of slavery, namely that blacks lacked intellect and were therefore not fully human beings. If pro-slavery pamphleteers were anxious to denigrate black writing, the Abolitionists were equally eager to announce, celebrate and valorize black writers as evidence of the humanity of blacks. Thomas Clarkson for instance, citing Phyllis Wheatley and Ignatius Sancho, wrote that 'if the minds of the Africans were unbroken by slavery, if they had the *same* expectations in life as other people, and the same opportunities for improvement, either in the colonies or upon the coast, they would be equal in all the various branches of science to the Europeans, and that the argument that states them to be an inferior link of the chain of nature and designed for servitude, as far as it depends on the *inferiority* of their capacities, is wholly malevolent and false'. Given the humanity of blacks, evidenced by their intellectual capacities, slavery, the argument ran, was therefore an appalling and indecent institution. Black writers themselves were at the forefront of the attack on slavery, not only through their books, but in the active business of campaigning for Abolition. Equiano for instance, in 1772, when a black English friend was forcibly kidnapped and put on board a ship to be sold in the West Indies, speedily obtained a writ of *habeas corpus* and contacted Granville Sharp for help (Granville Sharp having by this time earned a reputation as the foremost Abolitionist of the day). When in 1783 news broke of the murder of 132 African slaves aboard the slave-ship *Zong*, it was Equiano who contacted Granville Sharp again to enlist his legal support. Equiano had meetings with the Quakers who in 1783 had established a Committee for the Abolition of Slavery, and he led several black delegations to the House of Commons to attend the Slavery debates. He was received by the Speaker of the House of Commons and by the Prime Minister, and had consultations with several M.P.'s. After the publication of his book, Equiano travelled widely throughout the Kingdom addressing Abolitionist meetings - in 1789, Birmingham; in 1790, Manchester,

Nottingham and Cambridge; in 1791, Dublin and Cork; in 1792, Scotland. He was, as Shyllon has written, 'the first nationalist leader of black people in Britain who stood uncompromisingly for black Manhood, Dignity and Freedom'. His book had a tremendous impact in arousing and shaping public opinion against slavery. One white fellow Abolitionist estimated that Equiano was 'a principal instrument in bringing about the motion for a repeal of the Slave act'. John Wesley, the founder of Methodism and a leading crusader against slavery, was deeply moved by Equiano's book - on his death bed, his strength and faculties failing, it was Equiano's book that he asked to be read aloud to him.

Equiano's Travels is a most powerful indictment of slavery in the literature of the period, surpassing in power anything that Wordsworth, Blake, Cowper and other Abolition writers produced. The power of Equiano's book resides in its personal account and vision of what it was like to be black in the eighteenth century. It has an inner quality about it, an inner and personal testimony, and it is this intimacy with experience, this first-hand quality, that makes it superior to, and more convincing than much of white Abolitionist literature. Abolition literature written by whites can be contrived, stylish, artistic - it uses rhetoric to appeal to the reader's emotions, and after a while can become stale, trite, tedious. Equiano's book is wholly different - what he does is to simply narrate the incidents in his life, and he lets these incidents speak for themselves. His prose is calm, self-restrained, and natural, it rarely swells with rhetorical passion or adopts postures of grief or outrage. What Equiano does instead is tell his story simply and naturally, without rhetorical embellishments and other obvious demonstrations of literary skill. And on top of this calmness and self-control is a humour that is remarkable, given the condition of slavery that his narrative describes. This survival of humour betokens the triumph of Equiano's *humanity* over the dehumanizing processes of slavery. A little instance of this humour occurs when Equiano relates a story of an accident aboard a ship on which he was a sailor -

> One day in our passage we met with an accident which was near burning the ship. A black cook, in melting some fat, overset the pan into the fire under the deck, which immediately began to blaze, and the flame went up very high under the foretop. With the fright the poor cook became almost white, and altogether speechless. Happily however we got the fire out without doing much mischief.

There are five aspects of Equiano's narrative which deserve special mention. Firstly, the defence of African society that Equiano offers the reader against the accumulated myths and negative constructions typical of white literature on Africa. The first two chapters of the book describe Equiano's early childhood in what is now called Nigeria. 'We are almost a nation of dancers, musicians and poets', Equiano explains of the culture of his people, describing the music and drama that they engaged in. The existence of a culture in Africa is firmly established. Equiano goes on to detail the economic, legal and social systems created by his people, and what emerges is a sense of order and civilized codes of behaviour. Take for instance the administration of justice:

> The elders or chief men decided disputes and punished crimes, for which purpose they always assembled together. The proceedings were generally short, and in most cases the law of retaliation prevailed. I remember a man was brought before my father and the other judges for kidnapping a boy, and although he was a son of a chief or a senator, he was condemned to make recompense by a man or woman slave. Adultery, however, was sometimes punished with slavery or death, a punishment which I believe is inflicted on it throughout most of the nations of Africa, so sacred among them is the honour of the marriage bed, and so jealous are they of the fidelity of their wives.

What such a passage yields is firstly, a sense of the equality of justice in Nigeria - even though the son of a chief, the offender still receives punishment for his crime; secondly a sense of the essential *morality* of the people - sexual fidelity is honoured, and promiscuity punishable by death. The strictness of this sexual code is quite contrary to European myths about the sexual incontinence of Africans. Other information that Equiano supplies to us, which contradicts European prejudice relates, for instance, to cleanliness of body and cleanliness of speech: 'Before we taste good food we always wash our hands: indeed our cleanliness on all occasions is extreme, but on this it is an indispensable ceremony ... We are totally unacquainted with strong or spirituous liquors, and our principal beverage is palm wine'. On the decency of language Equiano explains that 'I remember we never polluted the name of the object of our adoration; on the contrary it was always mentioned with the greatest reverence, and we were totally unacquainted with swearing and all those terms of abuse and reproach which find their way so readily and copiously into the language of more civilised people'. A final instance of Equiano's redemptive purpose (i.e. cleansing the African of the filth of European description) is his assertion of the beauty of blackness, whiteness being seen in his society as a disease: 'I remember while in Africa to have seen three negro children who were tawny, and another quite white, who were universally regarded by myself and the natives in general, as far as related to their complexions, as *deformed* '.

In his description of his land as a community of *shared* labour and *shared* rituals, agriculturally-based and self-sufficient, with no notion of money or commerce, Equiano is not being romantic, for he also exposes the evils of his society. Slavery for instance exists: people taken prisoner in war, or those convicted of adultery or some other malevolent crime, become slaves. But the system of slavery is, Equiano says, profoundly different from West Indian slavery - the slaves within his African community work equally beside their owners; their food, clothing and lodging were more or less identical to that of their owners. The degree of physical brutalization, psychological humiliation and commercial exploitation that typifies European slavery is wholly absent.

The second aspect of Equiano's book to be noted is that as he asserts the values of his own society, he simultaneously demolishes certain features of white society. For the first time we begin to see what black people thought of England, and of white people. Equiano's first encounter with whites serves only to reveal to him the indignity and squalor of white behaviour. Seized and thrown aboard a slave-ship when still a child, he is amazed at the savage way in which the whites looked and acted, and is shocked by their cruelty. He believes them to be savages and thinks that he is about to be eaten by these ugly, hideous creatures. 'We thought by this we should be eaten by these ugly men'. The squalor of the slave-ship that takes them to the West Indies is described in poignant detail, but there is unique revelation too of the more *creative* moments. The description of the horrible deaths aboard the slave-ship is juxtaposed with little insights into what black people saw on the journey. 'During our passage I first saw flying fishes, which surprised me very much', Equiano says, revealing that even in the midst of murder he still retained a curiosity and boyish sense of wonder. One day he peeps through the quadrant, an instrument that the white sailors used to make measurements: 'The clouds appeared to me to be land, which disappeared as they passed along. This heightened my wonder, and I was now more persuaded than ever that I was in another world and that everything about me was magic'. Equiano sees the whole business of slavery through a boy's naive eyes, and the innocence of the boy's observations yields a refreshingly vivid and convincing perspective on European savagery. On landing in Barbados the boy Equiano is again amazed at the hideous and primitive behaviour of the whites - 'On a signal given, as the beat of a drum, the buyers rush at once into the yard where the slaves are confined, and make choice of that parcel they like best. The noise and clamour with which this is attended and the eagerness visible in the countenance of the buyers serve not a little to increase the apprehensions of the terrified Africans'. Again, there is a reversed situation here, where it is civilized Africans who are terrified by the primitive savagery of white people. After Barbados, Equiano is taken to England where again he is surprised at the low behaviour and indecency of whites: 'I was astonished at the wisdom of the white people in all things I saw, but was amazed at their not sacrificing or making any offerings, and eating with unwashed hands, and touching the dead. I likewise could not help remarking the particular slenderness of their women, which I did not at first like, and I thought they were not so modest and shamefaced as the African women'. It is always the stupidity and indecency of whites which amaze Equiano. Later in the book he tells a story of how a ship on which he was a sailor was caught up in a storm. Instead of working to save their lives, the white sailors sit around and get drunk: 'I warned the people who were drinking and entreated them to embrace the moment of deliverance, nevertheless they persisted, as if not possessed of the least spark of reason'. This disappointment with white people is also one which James Gronniosaw shared. Gronniosaw, in his autobiography, tells of how as a slave in the West Indies he always dreamed of going to England. He had met some English missionaries and he thought that everyone in England was just as holy, learned, and kind. 'I had a vast inclination to visit England', Gronniosaw wrote, 'and wished continually that it would please Providence to make a clear way for me to see this island. I entertained a notion that if I could get to England, I should never more experience either cruelty or ingratitude, so that I was very desirous to get among Christians'. Gronniosaw comes in for a shock when he does land in England:

> I cannot describe my joy when we were within sight of Portsmouth. But I was astonished when we landed to hear the inhabitants of that place curse and swear and be otherwise profane. I expected to find nothing but goodness, gentleness and meekness in this Christian land, I then suffered great perplexities of mind. I enquired if any serious Christian people resided there; the woman I made this enquiry of answered me in the affirmative, and added that she was one of them. I was heartily glad to hear her say so. I thought I could give her my whole heart: she kept a public house. I deposited with all the money that I had not an immediate occasion for; as I thought it would be safer with her. - It was 25 guineas but 6 of them I desired her to lay out to the best advantage, to buy me some shirts, a hat and some other necessaries. I made her a present of a very handsome looking glass that I brought with me from Martinico, in order to recompence her for the trouble I had given her. I must do this woman the justice to acknowledge that she did lay out some little for my use, but the 19 guineas and part of the 6 guineas with my watch, she would not return, but denied that I ever gave it to her.

> I soon perceived that I was got among bad people, who defrauded me of my money and watch; and that all my promised happiness was blasted. I had no friend but GOD and I prayed to him earnestly. I could scarcely believe it possible that the place where so many eminent Christians had lived and preached could abound with so much wickedness and deceit. I thought it worse than *Sodom* (considering the great advantage they have) I cried like a child, and that almost continually.

The third striking aspect of Equiano's narrative is his description of the petty cruelty of whites towards blacks. Slaves, to maintain a sense of selfhood and dignity, would attempt to acquire personal possessions; a small boat perhaps, or a bag of oranges, or a few coins. These possessions, of little financial worth, had great symbolic value: by owning independent property, the slaves, who were themselves dependent property, could lay for themselves the foundations of freedom. Their aspirations, however, were constantly thwarted by the whites who would simply take away these possessions. Equiano relates many instances of the humiliation of blacks by petty acts of white bullying. The true brutality of slavery lay not only with extravagant deeds of rape and slaughter perpetrated by whites against blacks, but in the little, nameless unremembered acts of unkindness and of contempt. These acts were a form of sadistic mental and spiritual torture - again and again the slaves are reduced to a state of nothingness, owning nothing for themselves, creating nothing for themselves.

The fourth aspect of black experience which is revealed by Equiano is the fierce desire to learn. Equiano has a thirst for knowledge, an intense curiosity towards the world about him. English literature was accustomed to presenting 'savages' awed by the artefacts of white culture.Friday fingers the compass or the gun of Crusoe with a sense of terror and puzzlement. He kneels before these implements as before new gods. Equiano, and the reality, was otherwise. Equiano's desire to learn is a natural, human urge. He has an open attitude to white culture, a willingness to take on board the best of that culture. His attitude is an isolated one, for the whites are not equally curious about black culture. They remain stubbornly and viciously narrow-minded. The act of mastery of white culture is also a life-saving strategy. His acquired sailing skills gain him money, authority and ultimately freedom. On many occasions, his command of the English language saves him from enslavement:

> This was not the only disagreeable incident I met with while I was in this place, for one day while I was a little way out of the town of Savannah, I was beset by two white men who meant to play their usual tricks with me in the way of kidnapping. As soon as these men accosted me, one of them said to the other, 'This is the very fellow we are looking

for that you lost:' and the other swore immediately that I was the identical person. On this they made up to me and were about to handle me, but I told them to be still and keep off, for I had seen those kind of tricks played upon other free blacks and they must not think to serve me so. At this they paused a little, and one said to the other - 'It will not do;' and the other answered that I talked too good English. I replied, I believed I did, and I had also with me a revengeful stick equal to the occasion, and my mind was likewise good. Happily however it was not used, and after we had talked together a little in this manner the rogues left me.

Finally, the desire to be loved. Equiano is loyal and devoted to anyone who shows him kindness and affection. In a life of constant uncertainty and cruelty, any token of kindness had to be seized upon. An owner who did not beat or cheat his/her slaves would be shown affection, sometimes lasting devotion, for the alternative was to end up being owned by someone more sadistic. Survival demanded a strategy of exhibiting affection and devotion. Apologists for slavery misinterpreted such devotion, arguing that blacks wanted to be slaves, that they were happily docile in the service of their masters and mistresses. Equiano's testimony offers more subtle and poignant insight into a psychology of dependence based on the measure of kindness received in the midst of general cruelty.

Major Texts

1. Ignatius Sancho *Letters of the Late Ignatius Sancho, an African* (London: 1782, Reprinted by Dawsons of Pall Mall, ed. Paul Edwards, 1968).

Ignatius Sancho was the first black prose writer to be published in England. Sancho was born in 1729 in mid-Atlantic, on board a slave-ship. His mother died soon afterwards, and his father committed suicide in preference to a life of slavery. Sancho was brought to England to be given as a gift to some English ladies. The Duke of Montagu took a liking to him. Under Montagu's patronage, Sancho acquired a classical education. During his life he wrote poetry, two stage plays and classical music. He became friendly with Gainsborough (who painted his portrait), Samuel Johnson, Laurence Sterne, John Hamilton Mortimer and other artists and writers of the day.

Sancho's letters, written in the style of Sterne's prose, were enormously popular. The first edition attracted over 1,200 subscribers, and as Peter Fryer informs us, this subscription figure was larger than any other publication of the century since *The Spectator*. The book was cited by Abolition sympathisers as evidence of the African's intellect and humanity. 'Let it no longer be said by half-informed philosophers, and superficial investigators of human nature, that *Negers*, as they are vulgarly called, are inferior to any white nation in mental abilities.'

A wide range of matters is covered in Sancho's letters. They deal with the warmth of friendships, the day-to-day business of the family (Sancho ran a grocer's shop in London), the racism and cruelty of some whites, and so on. They also comment in very interesting ways on English manners and behaviour, thus presenting the reader with a rare black perspective on England.

2. Ottobah Cugoano *Thoughts and sentiments on the evil and wicked traffic of the Slavery and Commerce of the human species* (London: 1787; Reprinted by Dawsons of Pall Mall, 1969)

Cugoano, born around 1757 in West Africa (in a region now called Ghana) was seized by slavers and shipped to Grenada. After nearly two years' servitude in the West Indies, he was taken to England by his owner, and eventually set free. In 1787 he published his powerful denunciation of the slave trade, with the help of his friend Equiano. In it he indicted the whole nation, from commoner to nobleman, for its inhumanity, and stoutly defended the slave's right to rebel (if necessary, by violence) against his/her oppressor. He exposed the hypocrisy of the British who, whilst claiming to be 'the most learned and civilized people in the world', in reality indulged in atrocities and genocide. Of the suffering of Africans at the hands of the British he wrote, 'Our lives are accounted of no value, we are hunted after as prey in the desert, and doomed to destruction as the beasts that perish.' If he argued against slavery, Cugoano proposed simultaneously a system of just trade with the blacks in the West Indies, for the economic benefit of both Europeans and blacks.

3. Phyllis Wheatley *Poems on various subjects, religious and moral* (London, 1773; new edition published by the University of North Carolina Press, 1966)

Although Wheatley spent all her life in Boston, her brief visit to England in 1773, and the subsequent publication in London of her book of poems, were important contributions to anti-slavery sentiment in this country. As one historian put it, she was 'a supreme witness to the anti-slavery movement in Britain'.

Wheatley, owned by a Boston tailor's wife, was a remarkable child, and one of the few black slaves who were given the opportunity to learn to read and write, on account of her exceptional talents. She not only mastered English but was fluent in Latin. Her owner, 'proud' of her exceptional slave, encouraged the process of learning.

Wheatley attracted much attention in her visit to London, and the aristocracy, always excited by the novel or the curious, flocked to see her. 'The Lord Mayor of London presented her with a valuable edition of Milton's *Paradise Lost*', Peter Fryer informs us (Peter Fryer, *Staying Power*, 1984, p. 92). On a serious level her book was used to argue for the abolition of slavery. A reviewer in the *Monthly Review* of 1773 expressed concern that such a fine and talented human being should suffer enslavement.

For all her fame, Wheatley died in America, in abject poverty, in 1784, at the age of 30.

4. Ukawsaw Gronniosaw *A Narrative of the most remarkable particulars in the life of James Albert Ukawsaw Gronniosaw, an African prince, as related by himself* (Bath, c.1770).

Born a prince in Borno (a region in present-day Nigeria), Gronniosaw was enslaved as a boy in the West Indies, then America. He was freed upon the death of his owner, and after a series of jobs (cook, soldier, servant) ended up in England. His life in England was one of severe hardship. He married a poor white woman, Betty, and, together with their three children, eked out a meagre living in a variety of odd jobs, sometimes existing at the edge of starvation. He had come to England with great expectations of making a good living in a Christian land, but ended up in failure and distress:

> Such is our situation at present.- My wife, by hard labour at the loom, does every thing that can be expected from her, towards the maintenance of our family, and GOD is pleased to incline the hearts of his people at times to yield us their charitable assistance, being myself through age and infirmities able to contribute but little to their support.

5. John Jea *The Life, History and Unparalleled Sufferings of John Jea, African Preacher of the Gospel* (Portsmouth, c. 1814)

A former slave in America, Jea ended up as an itinerant Methodist preacher in America and Britain. His autobiography gives little information on his African ancestry, filled as it is with snippets of sermons, moral reflections and quotations from the Bible. Nor is it clear at what date he arrived in Britain. Whilst in Britain he travelled throughout the Kingdom preaching to packed congregations. Such was his popularity in Ireland that the Catholic establishment threatened his life and he had to seek the protection of the army. Jea apparently ended up in Portsea, where, apart from his autobiography, he published a hymn-book. Both publications are soon to be reprinted by Oxford University Press under the editorship of David Dabydeen and a team of Yale University scholars headed by Henry Gates.

B. Women Writers: Mary Seacole's *Wonderful Adventures of Mrs Seacole in many lands* (1857; Reprinted in 1984 by Falling Wall Press)

Black women have been living in Britain at least since the early sixteenth century, the earliest written records telling of a group of young women in Scotland, in the court of James IV. We know very little of their origins or life but judging from the documents on court experience these black women were richly apparelled, their sartorial elegance indicating that they were part of the aristocratic environment of music, banquetting and tournament games. The overwhelming experience of black women in Britain, however, has been less glamorous than that of courtly entertainment. In the seventeenth and eighteenth centuries the records point to employment as domestic servants, seamstresses, laundry-maids, children's nurses, fair-ground performers and so on. Many were forced into street prostitution, some like 'Black Harriot' becoming famous courtesans (it was said that her numerous clients included 20 members of the House of Lords). Unlike Equiano, Sancho *et al.*, they left no written records of their life's experience, this due to lack of access to a literary education. Phyllis Wheatley was an American who spent a short time in Britain; there were no female black British writers in the eighteenth century who had spent a large part of their lives in Britain. Apart from the writings of Mary Prince, whose autobiography was published in Edinburgh in 1831 (*The History of Mary Prince, a West Indian Slave*), and of Mary Seacole, scholars have not yet uncovered any other publication of black British women of the nineteenth century.

Mary Seacole, the daughter of a Scottish army officer and a free black woman, was born in Jamaica in 1805, 29 years *before* the Abolition of Slavery. Her claim to fame lay in her services as a nurse to the British Army during the Crimean war, services which made her a household name. In 1857, a benefit Festival was held in the Royal Surrey Gardens in her honour, taking place over four consecutive nights, with over 40,000 people. The *Times* of 28 and 30 July 1857 reporting the occasion wrote:

Nothing could have been more triumphantly successful ... Notwithstanding that the charge for admission was quintupled, there was an immense concourse in the hall. Mrs. Seacole sat in state in front of the centre gallery, supported by Lord Rokeby on one side, by Lord George Paget on the other, and surrounded by the members of her committee ... Few names were more familiar to the public during the late war than that of Mrs. Seacole ... At the end of both the first and second parts the name of Mrs. Seacole was shouted by a thousand voices. The genial old lady rose from her place and smiled benignantly on the assembled multitude, amid a tremendous and continued cheering. Never did woman seem happier, and never was hearty and kindly greeting bestowed upon a worthier object ... on no previous occasion have the Royal Surrey Gardens been thronged by a greater multitude. The music-hall was literally crammed, many hundreds of persons being compelled to remain in the grounds, unable to penetrate into the interior of the building.

In the same month, July 1857, Mary Seacole published her autobiography, which was an instant success, and which was reprinted within the year. When Mary Seacole died in 1881, she left an estate valued at £ 2,615 - a relatively substantial sum, the equivalent of tens of thousands of pounds today. No less a newspaper than the *Times* announced her death: previously, a variety of newspapers, including the *London Advertiser* and the *Illustrated London News,* had carried accounts of her life and work, and *Punch* published a poem in her honour. Although totally forgotten by the twentieth century British public (in contrast to Florence Nightingale, the other heroine of the Crimea), Mary Seacole remains one of the most significant women of her times. She was extraordinary in terms of her fame and the respect she commanded from British nobility and commoner alike.

Mary Seacole learnt folk medicine from her mother who was something of a nurse, and she became skilled at treating tropical diseases like cholera and yellow fever. She practiced her skills in Jamaica, then in Panama and Columbia saving many lives and earning the gratitude of many. In 1853 war broke out between Britain and Russia, and in 1854, Britain and France sent troops to the Crimea in defence of the Russian invasion of the Turkish Empire. Mary Seacole set off for London in 1854, then moved to the Crimea where she set up a hotel, the *British Hotel,* to cater for

British officers, and she spent much time on the battlefield, nursing the wounded and the dying.

This saintliness on the part of Seacole is undermined by her patriotic and romantic glorification of war. Telling us about her ambition to go to the Crimea to help the British cause she says, 'what delight should I not experience if I could be useful to my own "sons", suffering for a cause it was so glorious to fight and bleed for!' She describes war as a dashing and colourful event:

> We saw the Russians fall slowly back in good order, while the dark-plumed Sardinians and red-pantalooned French spread out in pursuit, and formed a picture so excitingly beautiful that we forgot the suffering and death they left behind.

Here is her spontaneous reaction on first seeing a battle:

> My first experience of battle was pleasant enough ... It was very pretty to see the advance and to watch how every now and then little clouds of white smoke puffed up from behind bushes and crests of hills, and were answered by similar puffs from the long line of busy skirmishers that preceded the main body. This was my first experience of actual battle, and I felt that strange excitement which I do not remember on future occasions, coupled with an earnest longing to see more of warfare, and to share in its hazards. It was not long before my wish was gratified.

Some of her descriptions of the injuries suffered by the soldiers are also full of pomp and circumstance. She depicts the common soldiers as full of patriotic bravado and heroism - one soldier for instance, his leg blown away, is still full of spirit and cheerful and impatient to get back into battle to die for King and Country! In another passage she describes an officer's servant 'lying crouched in a rifle pit, having "pots" at the Russians, or keeping watch in the long line of trenches, or, stripped to his shirt shovelling powder and shot into the great guns, whose steady roar broke the evening's calm'. The poetic language (alliteration and rhythm are brilliantly employed in the sentence) no doubt stirred the patriotic emotions of the book's readership.

Underlying all these descriptions of romantic heroism is Mary Seacole's own enduring patriotism. Her devotion to Queen and Country is a dominant feature of the narrative. She speaks proudly of the 'part she bore of the trials and hardships endured on that distant shore, where Britain's best and bravest wrung hardy Sebastapol from the grasp of Britain's foe'. This patriotism is at times embarrassing and gauche. She attends the funeral of Lord Raglan, the Commander in Chief of the British Army, 'that great soldier who had such iron courage', and at the funeral, proudly and sadly she touches the Union Jack:

> And once again they let me into the room in which the coffin lay, and I timidly stretched out my hand and touched a corner of the union-jack which lay upon it, and then I watched it wind its way through the long lines of soldiery towards Kamiesch, while, ever and anon, the guns thundered forth in sorrow. And for days after I could not help thinking of the ship which was ploughing its way through the sunny sea with its sad burden.

Again we note the poetic nature of the prose, its use of alliteration to heighten the emotion and to bind the sentences together into a measured lament.

All this patriotic rhetoric and fervour is curious given the fact of Seacole's colour, given the rampant racism of the English towards the blacks in their midst, given the plundering and partitioning of Africa that was being undertaken by Europeans and given the colonial repression in Jamaica which had only just emerged from Slavery. Mary Seacole, however, in her religious fervour, her moral outlook (she banned gambling and drinking in her British Hotel in the Crimea) and her militaristic patriotism, is an imperial and Victorian figure, though ludicrously so because of her colour. Seacole indeed relished the fact that she was a servant of Empire. She proudly cites a letter of tribute she received from an officer who said, 'I am sure that when her Gracious Majesty the Queen shall have become acquainted with the service you have rendered to so many of her brave soldiers, her generous heart will thank you. For you have been an instrument in the hands of the Almighty to preserve many a gallant heart to the Empire, to fight and win her battles, if ever again war may become a necessity.' Seacole loved such praise. Indeed, when the Crimean War was over, she set her mind to go to India to serve the British army there against the rebellious hordes of savage natives. 'Give me my needle and thread, my medicine chest, my bandages, my probe and scissors, and I am off to India' she declared to the British Secretary of War. Fortunately for the Indians Seacole changed her mind.

137

It is true that Mary Seacole received racial insults during her lifetime, on account of her colour, as a result of which she defends black people against the racist ideas of whites, and exhibits a pride in African achievement. She is proud of the fact that many free Africans in Latin America became civic leaders, government officials, magistrates, and so on. Although many in white society saw Seacole as a 'nigger', she is more ambivalent about her colour. She was proud that she was half-white. On the first page of her narrative she declares that the better half of her character is due to her white ancestry:

> I am a Creole, and have good Scotch blood coursing through my veins. Many people have traced to my Scottish blood that energy and activity which are not always found in the Creole race, and which have carried me to so many varied scenes: and perhaps they are right.

One white contemporary said of her 'She told me that she had Scotch blood in her veins. I must say that she did not look like it, but the old lady spoke proudly of this point in her genealogy'. Throughout the narrative Mrs. Seacole proudly refers to herself as a 'yellow woman' or a 'brown woman'. Indeed she can sometimes exhibit a vicious contempt for black people (whom she calls 'niggers') and for all non-British nationalities. Her stereotypical descriptions of Greeks, Maltese and Turks would have appealed to the xenophobia of a Victorian reading public. She speaks of the 'lazy Maltese', of 'cunning-eyed Greeks', dismisses Turks as 'deliberate, slow and indolent', and Spanish Indians as 'treacherous, passionate and indolent, with no higher aim or object but simply to enjoy the present after their own torpid, useless fashion'.

Seacole's patriotism, and her attitude to race, reveal a split personality. On the one hand, she is sensitive to a black ancestry and sensitive to the racism directed against blacks. On the other, she shows contempt for blacks, and non-British peoples, and is happy to declare her half-whiteness. Her narrative yields unique insight into the divided loyalties of colonial people of mixed blood and heritage.

Major Texts

1. Grace Nichols *I is a Long Memoried Woman* (London: Caribbean Cultural International, 1983; London: Karnak House Publication, 1983).

A first collection by a Guyanese-born poet which deservedly won the Commonwealth Poetry Prize, 1983. The poems chart the movement from Africa to the Caribbean, revealing the processes of suffering and psychological breakdown, but the final defiant endurance of the black woman over the barbarism of history. Nichols's verse can be beautifully crafted, her technical command of both English and creole language indicating a poet of considerable ability:

> Heavy with child
>
> belly
> an arc
> of black moon
>
> I squat over
> dry plantain leaves
>
> and command the earth
> to receive you
>
> in my name
> in my blood
>
> to receive you
> my curled bean
>
> my tainted
>
> perfect child
>
> my bastard fruit
> my seedling
> my sea grape
> my strange mulatto
> my little bloodling

2. Buchi Emecheta *Second-Class Citizen* (London: Fontana, 1974)

The story of Adah, a Nigerian-born woman who emigrates to England to join her husband Francis. The novel deals with the cruel racism of English society. Her expectations of a happy and comfortable existence in England are shattered by the cold welcome she receives at the outset:

> England gave Adah a cold welcome. The welcome was particularly cold because only a few days previously they had been enjoying bright and cheerful welcomes from ports like Takoradi, Freetown and Las Palmas. If Adah had been Jesus, she would have passed England by. Liverpool was grey, smoky and looked uninhabited by humans. It reminded Adah of the loco-yard where they told her Pa had once worked as a moulder. In fact the architectural designs were the same. But if, as people said, there was plenty of money in England, why then did the natives give their visitors this poor cold welcome? Well, it was too late to moan, it was too late to change her mind. She could not have changed it even if she had wanted to. Her children must have an English education and, for that reason, she was prepared to bear the coldest welcome, even if it came from the land of her dreams.

Cramped living conditions, racial abuse and general poverty are her lot. She suffers too from the bullying and aggression of Francis who expresses his sense of failure through violent behaviour. All in all the black people in England are reduced to the status of animals, their squalid living conditions seriously undermining their humanity:

> The housing conditions were so bad that for days she didn't see Francis at all. As soon as she arrived home from work he would disappear for fresh air. The children had no amusements and their parents would not let them out for fear they would break their necks on the steep stairs. They were hushed and bullied into silence so that the landlord and his wife should not be disturbed. When it rained, which was often, the nappies were dried in the same room. The second-hand heater they used always smoked. The Obis lived not as human beings at all, but like animals.

The novel gives particular insight into the female condition. The passages describing Adah's stay in the maternity ward, and her problems with the contraceptive coil, show Emecheta's concern with experiences of crucial relevance to women. Adah is the 'other' in two ways - as a black person, and as a woman.

3. Joan Riley, *The Unbelonging* (London: The Woman's Press, 1985)

A black novel describing the physical and mental traumas in the life of a black girl in England. Hyacinth, emigrating from Jamaica, suffers a loss of self-confidence because of her colour; in a society where 'whiteness' is the basis of acceptable beauty, she feels ugly and contemptuous of herself. 'Sometimes in her secret fantasies she would be swept off her feet by a rich, passionate stranger ... Always her hair would be blonde and flowing, her skin pale and white'. Her unhappy experience of English school-life, one of loneliness and racial aggression, is compounded by her father's cruel and perverse behaviour and his sexual intentions towards her. She retreats from the world of brutality through daydreaming and fantasy, creating in her mind an image of her childhood homeland (Jamaica) as a haven of innocence. 'Only the thought of Jamaica sustained her'. Her eventual return to Jamaica however is harrowing. The reality of grime, disorder and menace overwhelms her, she feels deeply alienated, deeply lonely. She has no 'home'. The novel ends on a bleak note suggesting her psychological disorientation and retreat into herself.

4. Amryl Johnson, *Long Road to Nowhere* (London: Virago Press, 1985).

A book of poems which evoke life in Trinidad and Tobago,from the frolic of steelband to the grime of city slums. The playing of pan, the 'swaying' and the 'jamming' emerge from an existence of suffering:

> The trail of dust which sifts
> up to the dirt road leads to where the earth
> is stone and breaks the hoe. The seeds
> cannot be coaxed in rain which
> does not come
> You walk away with callous
> hands, defeat

This paradox is explored memorably in 'The New Cargo Ship', where the layers of history are shuffled and where the identities of those who people history converge:

They came out of the belly of their suffering
into
the new cargo ship
joyful
singing songs
drinking rum
radios blaring
on the sea
once their enemy
This boat is crammed
as it was then
Still travelling
        in transit
always in transit
And the young man who led
the rebellion is now
the old man
in the red shirt
high with fervour
singing with feverish enthusiasm
drunk on whisky
drunk with disillusion
The one whose stomach heaves
with every wave
was the one who threw
himself overboard when
he could take no more
A people on the waves
        of the waves
And where was I in all this?
Where was I?

As with Grace Nichols and several other young poets, Johnson's first book of poems is overwhelmingly a recollection of a West Indian childhood or background. It is as if England cannot be directly written about until the West Indian experience is first expressed. England is,however, an unspoken presence in their poetry: England is the cold, adult, alienating experience which gives the life to passionate recollection of West Indian childhood memories.

5. *A Dangerous Knowing: Four Black Women Poets* (London: Sheba Feminist Publishers, n.d.)

A selection of poems by Grace Nichols, Barbara Burford, Gabriela Pearse and Jackie Kay, on diverse topics such as childbirth, schooldays, family life and feminism. All the writers are concerned with their dual identities as black people and as women. The relation between black and white women is also examined, as the titles of some of the poems reveal: 'We are not all sisters under the same moon'; 'We the Women'. The best of these is Nichols' 'Between Women':

> We recognise each other
> exhilarate in the recognition
> of each other
> across the kitchen table
> we spend hours
> reclaiming
> obscured from history our mothers
> talk about our fondness
> for our wombs and lovers
>
> Disappoint
> we disappoint each other
> use and betray
> use and betray each other
> sometimes we even choose
> to kill each other
>
> But the need to fill
> the pages of silence between us
> remain

C. The Immigrant Experience: Samuel Selvon's
The Lonely Londoners (1956)

The early writings of Equiano, Sancho, Seacole and others, whilst constituting a mere handful of books, nevertheless reveal black literary concern with the issues of racism, and its effect on community and on the individual personality. All the early writers are compelled to argue their humanity, the fact that they belong to the human species, for, as black people, they had been excluded from consideration as human beings. They show their white readership human qualities of intelligence, morality, compassion and courage as being essential features of their individuality and of their community. The bulk of black British writing takes place this century, with the new immigration of the post-*Windrush* era, but the issue of humanity remains a crucial concern. The struggle to thwart fascist concepts of 'otherness' remains a central responsibility of the new writers.

The Lonely Londoners deals with the shattering of the illusion of belonging, the illusion of being English, and indeed the illusion about who the English are. The journey to England is a journey to an illusion, and the sojourn in England is a shattering of that illusion. The illusion is, firstly, a material dream about the wealth of England - the streets are meant to be paved with gold, with work well-paid and readily available. Secondly, it is an illusion about the courtesy, hospitality and human warmth of the English. This illusory hospitality of the English involves an imagined willingness of their white women to readily accept black men. As Galahad reveals on the eve of his first date with a white woman,

> This was something he used to dream about in Trinidad. The time when he was leaving, Frank tell him: 'Boy, it have bags of white pussy in London, and you will eat till you tired' And now, the first date, in the heart of London, dressed to kill, ready to escort the number around the town, anywhere she want to go, any place at all.

Finally the illusion of England involves a romantic sense of English history. Names like Charing Cross, Waterloo and Trafalgar Square are powerfully seductive:

He had a way, whenever he talking with the boys, he using the names of the places like they mean big romance, as if to say 'I was in Oxford Street' have more prestige than if he just say 'I was up the road.' And once he had a date with a frauline, and he make a big point of saying he was meeting she by Charing Cross, because just to say 'Charing Cross' have a lot of romance in it, he remember it had a song called 'Roseann of Charing Cross.' So this is how he getting on to Moses:

'I meeting that piece of skin tonight, you know.' And then, as if it not very important, 'She waiting for me by Charing Cross Station.'

Jesus Christ, when he say 'Charing Cross,' when he realise that is he, Sir Galahad, who going there, near that place that everybody in the world know about (it even have the name in the dictionary) he feel like a new man. It didn't matter about the woman he going to meet, just to say he was going there made him feel big and important, and even if he was just going to coast a lime, to stand up and watch the white people, still, it would have been something.

The seduction of England is the illusion of its romantic or fabulous history, and the illusion that the West Indian could participate in that history. It was a powerful dream especially since West Indians were taught, through colonial education, that there was no history or romance or fable in the islands; that all history resided in England.

In the novel, all the dreams are painfully destroyed by the reality of their encounter with the actual England. The theme of illusion and reality or dream and awakening, is central to the novel, and it is for this reason Moses is its central character. Moses is in a sense the leader or head of the West Indian group. 'Every Sunday morning, like if they going to church, the boys liming in Moses room, coming together for a oldtalk, to find out the latest gen, what happening, when is the next fête, Burt asking is anyone see his girl anywhere, Cap recounting an episode he had with a woman... Always every Sunday they coming to Moses, like if is confession, sitting down on the bed, on the floor, on the chairs.' The references to 'church' and 'confession' endow Moses with religious significance. A paragraph later, Selvon shifts the action to the Embankment, and we see Moses, a solitary figure, staring at the river, brooding on his fate and the fate of his fellow West Indians:

The old Moses, standing on the banks of the Thames. Sometimes he think he see some sort of profound realisation in his life, as if all that

145

happen to him is experience that make him a better man, as if now he could draw apart from any hustling and just sit down and watch other people fight to live. Under the kiff-kiff laughter, behind the ballad and the episode, the what-happening, the summer-is-hearts, he could see a great aimlessness, a great restless, swaying movement that leaving you standing in the same spot. As if a forlorn shadow of doom fall on all the spades in the country.

This picture of 'old Moses standing on the banks of the Thames' on the brink of vision, alludes to the Biblical Moses on the banks of the Nile, brooding on the fate of his people in bondage, his people stranded in a foreign land, and brooding on the possibility of Exodus and of locating the Promised Land. This linking of Moses and the Biblical Moses reinforces the novel's theme of the dream or illusion of Utopia and the reality of bondage. The crucial difference between Selvon's Moses and the Biblical Moses is that Selvon's Moses, and his fellow West Indians, have no place to go, no Promised Land to inherit. England is not the Promised Land, as previously thought, and poverty prevents them going back - they can't even raise the boat-fares to return to the West Indies. In any case they still hold out a hope that things in England will get better, or else they cannot wholly shake off the illusion or dream of England's possibilities. So they remain, they try to establish some roots, they try to live themselves into the history of the place. When Moses meets Harris and Galahad their conversation reveals both rootlessness and a craving for roots:

Hello boy, what happening.
So what happening, man, what happening.
How long you in Brit'n boy?
You think this winter bad? You should of been here in '52.
What happening, what happening man.

Harris, by referring back to the winter of '52 is indicating that he is now a part of the history of the place, part of the national memory, as opposed to newcomers like Galahad who have yet to lay down historical roots. This craving for identification with English history, this desire to belong and to participate in the making of English history, remains to the very end. Hence, in the closing pages of the novel, Moses broods again on the history of England:

The changing of the seasons, the cold slicing winds, the falling leaves, sunlight on green grass, snow on the land, London particular. Oh what it is and where it is and why it is, no one knows, but to have said: 'I walked on Waterloo Bridge,' 'I rendezvoused at Charing Cross,' 'Piccadilly Circus is my playground,' to say these things, to have lived these things, to have lived in the great city of London, centre of the world. To one day lean against the wind walking up the Bayswater Road (destination unknown), to see the leaves swirl and dance and spin on the pavement (sight unseeing), to write a casual letter home beginning: 'Last night, in Trafalgar Square...'

Moses, however, is finally unrelated to the history because white society does not allow West Indian participation in the present, nor does it recognise the West Indian dimension in its past history. The West Indian is thus stranded in England, physically and spiritually. This alienation is poignantly related in the story of Galahad's first outing in London, when he gets lost and suddenly feels wholly estranged, wholly alone:

Galahad make for the tube station when he left Moses, and he stand up there on Queensway watching everybody going about their business, and a feeling of loneliness and fright come on him all of a sudden. He forget all the brave words he was talking to Moses, and he realise that here he is, in London, and he ain't have money or work or place to sleep or any friend or anything, and he standing up here by the tube station watching people, and everybody look so busy he frighten to ask questions from any of them. You think any of them bothering with what going on in his mind? Or in anybody else mind but their own? He see a test come and take a newspaper and put down the money on a box - nobody there to watch the fellar and yet he put the money down. What sort of thing is that? Galahad wonder, they not afraid somebody thief the money?

He bounce up against a woman coming out the station but she pass him like a full trolley before he could say sorry. Everybody doing something or going somewhere, is only he who walking stupid.

On top of that, is one of those winter mornings when a kind of fog hovering around. The sun shining, but Galahad never see the sun look like how it looking now. No heat from it, it just there in the sky like a force-ripe orange. When he look up, the colour of the sky so desolate it make him more frighten. It have a kind of melancholy aspect about the morning that making him shiver. He have a feeling is about seven o'clock in the evening: when he look at a clock on top a building he see is only half-past ten in the morning.

The coldness of the English weather, matched by the coldness of the people, and strangeness of their streets, leaves Galahad in a state of *loneliness*. The illusion of England as being hospitable and warm, in human terms, and familiar in terms of the sense of Britishness that West Indians possessed in the colonies, suddenly dissolves and panic sets in.

The disappointment with England takes many forms - the West Indians are faced with outright discrimination in housing and employment, and grinding poverty which forces them to eat pigeons snatched secretly from public parks. And the white women they dreamt of turn out to be common sluts and old prostitutes, and possession of these women provides no entry into white society. Bart for instance, a light-skinned Trinidadian goes out with an ex-prostitute, telling her that he is a Latin-American, that he comes from South America (he is ashamed of his West Indian background), but he is still chased from his girlfriend's house by her father. When she leaves him, he spends the rest of his time walking all over London, peering into buses, trains, tubes, to find her, until be becomes haggard and haunted. But the illusion has gone forever, he never finds her again.

Bart's madness is one that afflicts the other West Indians in different forms, Selvon's concern being to explore the *psychology* of deracination, disappointment and rejection. We are told of a Jamaican fellow who breaks down as the pressures of poverty and disappointment build up, and suddenly goes mad in the dole office, tearing up the files, and beating up the officers, until the police come and take him away. But the experience of dislocation and alienation is most powerfully expressed in the incident where Galahad examines his skin, having just been insulted as a black bastard by two white men:

> And Galahad would take his hand from under the blanket, as he lay there studying how the night before he was in the lavatory and two white fellars come in and say how these black bastards have the lavatory dirty, and they didn't know that he was there, and when he come out they say hello mate have a cigarette. And Galahad watch the colour of his hand, and talk to it, saying, 'Colour, is you that causing all this, you know. Why the hell you can't be blue, or red or green, if you can't be white? You know is you that cause a lot of misery in the world. Is not me, you know, is you! I ain't do anything to infuriate the people and them is

you! Look at you, you so black and innocent, and this time so you causing misery all over the world!' So Galahad talking to the colour Black, as if is a person, telling it that is not *he* who causing botheration in the place, but Black, who is a worthless thing for making trouble all about. 'Black you see what you cause to happen yesterday? I went to look at that room that Ram tell me about in the Gate, and as soon as the landlady see you she say the room let already. She ain't even give me a chance to say good morning. Why the hell you can't change colour?'

Beneath the comedy is Selvon's exploration of the separation of self from body, the divorce of personality from flesh, that racism effects. The West Indian finally becomes schizophrenic under the pressure of racism.

Major Texts

1. J.D. Douglas *'Me Ago England' and 'Culture' (Caribbean Man's Blues,* Akira Press, 1985).

'Me Ago England' outlines certain illusions of the West Indian immigrant. He leaves behind a life of poverty and violence, a life of 'fighting for survival', thinking to find in England material wealth and 'progress'

> Me go bank me money
> me go get rich quick
> put it in a business fur me little pickney

England is the 'Motherland', 'head of de Commonwealth', and the immigrant expects to benefit from this parenthood. There is a child-like expectancy of a life of simple pleasures in England:

> Me ago Mother Land
> me ago Birmingham
> gonna build me a snow man, in de winter time.

'Culture' is set a generation after, describing the loss of values involved in the process of integration into England. The child of the immigrant is ignorant of ancestral culture. He 'knows of Hitler and Mussolini' but 'never heard about Marcus Garvey'. If he is intellectually deprived of black philosophical perspectives, his routine existence is also banal, rooted exclusively in the trash of England: 'His favourite food is fish and chips'; 'He plays football, supports West Ham'; 'He's British of course'. Although both poems are badly crafted, unsubtle and insensitive to the poetic potential of creole, they usefully reveal an opinion on the immigrant experience from a younger-generation black writer.

2. Wole Soyinka 'Telephone Conversation' in *Voices*, ed. Geoffrey Summerfield (Harmondsworth, Penguin Books, 1968)

A brilliant poem on the effects of racism on forcing a black person into self-consciousness. Soyinka, looking for a room, is questioned on the telephone by a landlady, and forced to become aware of, to examine and to evaluate, the colour of his body.

> Considerate she was, varying the emphasis -
> 'ARE YOU DARK? OR VERY LIGHT?' Revelation came.
> 'You mean - like plain or milk chocolate?'
> Her assent was clinical, crushing in its light
> Impersonality. Rapidly, wave-length adjusted,
> I chose. 'West African sepia' - and as an afterthought,
> 'Down in my passport.' Silence for spectroscopic
> Flight of fancy, till truthfulness changed her accent
> Hard on the mouthpiece. 'WHAT'S THAT?' conceding
> 'DON'T KNOW WHAT THAT IS.' 'Like brunette.'
> 'THAT'S DARK, ISN'T IT?' 'Not altogether.
> Facially, I am brunette, but, madam, you should see
> The rest of me. Palm of my hand, soles of my feet
> Are a peroxide blond. Friction, caused -
> Foolishly, madam - by sitting down, has turned
> My bottom raven black - One moment, madam!' - sensing
> Her receiver rearing on the thunderclap
> About my ears - 'Madam', I pleaded, 'wouldn't you rather
> See for yourself?'

The staccato ordering of the sentences conveys the nature of a telephone conversation between strangers, but more pertinently, it captures the confusion of mind as Soyinka rapidly has to assess his colour in relation to his personality. Soyinka's authorial voice speaks over his voice to the landlady, this duality paralleling the severance between spirit and flesh: his intellect is forced to contemplate the colour of his skin as a separate entity from his total person.

3. Jimi Rand 'A Black Man's Song' in *News for Babylon,* ed. J. Berry (London: Chatto and Windus, 1984)

Rand, using a nursery-rhyme form, and alluding to a fairy-tale ('Mirror, mirror on the wall / who is the fairest of them all?'), explores his identity in relation to his physical appearance:

> I looked in the mirror
> What did I see?
> Not black, not white,
> But me, only me.

The repetition of 'me', with the added charge of 'only', hint at a desperation in Rand to assert his being irrespective of colour. True, the 'me' has physical proportions, but Rand is saying that physique betokens no particular or peculiar human qualities. Physical racial characteristics are of no significance whatsoever. Indeed, Rand's body is not the 'African' body, but his own:

> Coal black face
> with big bright eyes
> and lilywhite teeth
> that's lil old me.

It is a remarkable poem which, with child-like naivety (through the deliberate use of nursery rhyme) asks complex questions about race and individuality, spirit and body.

4. John Agard 'Palm Tree King' and 'Stereotype' in *Mangoes and Bullets,* (London: Pluto Press, 1984)

A wonderful comic exposure of the philistine ignorance of the English, and their simplistic views of West Indian life. The West Indian individual is caught up in English racial stereotypes and generalizations. He is associated with palm trees, beaches, cricket, jungle drums, calypso. Agard's scorn is directed against the white tourist mentality that reduces landscape to pleasure-park and the West Indian individual to a figure of entertainment. The humanity of the West Indian is lost in this process of simplification.

5. Linton Kwesi Johnson 'Five Nights of Bleeding' in *Dread Beat and Blood* (London: Bogle L'Ouverture Publications, 1974)

'madness ... madness ... war' is the refrain of a poem which conveys with terrible insight and feeling the pressures of physical and psychological disintegration. Black existence in Britain is racked by violence and disorder. In a packed dance hall violence erupts like madness, and the music breeds and sustains the murderous passion:

> night number one was in BRIXTON:
> SOFRANO B sound system
> was a beating out a rhythm with a fire,
> coming doun his reggae-reggae wire;
> it was a sound shaking doun your spinal column,
> a bad music tearing up your flesh;
> and the rebels them start a fighting,
> the yout them jus turn wild.
> it's war amongst the rebels:
> madness ... madness ... war.

Johnson's gift as a poet is his ability to convey dread and terror; to describe the human personality in torment and self-destruction. A compassion for the victims of deprivation, for the under-class of the black community, accompanies the poet's sense of the terror of their behaviour and experience.

D. Violence

In June 1856, the Nawab of Bengal, resentful of encroaching British power in India, suddenly attacked the British garrison in Bengal. One hundred and forty six British captives were thrown into a military prison, known as the 'Black Hole', a room a mere 18 feet by 14 feet 10 inches. The next morning, there were only twenty-three survivors - the rest had perished through thirst, suffocation and madness. A year later, in May, 1857, the Indian army mutinied, turning its guns against its British officers. Massive civil rebellions were sparked off in many provinces in India, the disaffection arising out of native anger at British attempts to impose British values on India. Both sides indulged in atrocities; the rebels, on capturing a British-ruled town, would massacre its white population; the British, on taking a rebel stronghold would engage in mass executions - sometimes, several hundred Indians would be executed in one go by the British.

These examples of the bloodshed of Imperialism can be multiplied when considering the relationship between Africans and the British. The slave-trade involved a massive loss of life, as many as one-third of the slaves dying at sea. The slave plantations in the West Indies and the Americas were notorious for the savage treatment of African slaves. Slave rebellions - the most famous being Toussaist L'Ouverture's uprising against the French in Haiti - involved massacre and rape. The suppression of rebellion was undertaken through mass killings of the blacks. To cite but one such incident: in the Morant Bay riots of 1865, Governor Eyre of Jamaica ordered the execution not only of the leaders of the rebellion (Paul Bogle, George William Gordon and others) but also the killing of about six hundred rebels, and the flogging of a similar number.

Violence then, has been a characteristic, even dominant, aspect of black - white encounter for centuries. Such violence also typified race relations in Britain from the early days of the black presence in this country. An examination of seventeenth and eighteenth-century London newspapers indicates the violence suffered by black slaves in British households. These slaves frequently ran away, and the newspapers carried advertisements for their recapture:

> A Negro named Robert Moore about 18 years of age, of middle stature in Livery of Fawn-Coloured Cloth edg'd and lined with Crimson Bages, *having lost his thumb from his left hand*, went away from his master, Paul Nicol Esq: of Hendon in the County of Middlesex, on Sunday morning last, being the 22 instant and is suspected to have taken with him Goods of his Masters of a considerable value. Whoever apprehends him, and gives notice to his master at Hendon aforesaid, or to John Nicol Esq; at his house in White-Fryers, or to Mr. William Nicol

Woollen-draper at the Golden Fleece and Grace in Grace-Church-street,London, shall have 40s. Reward: and further satisfaction, if required.

(London Gazette, 23/6 April 1677)

Francis Smith, a middle sized black Man, about 30 years old ran away from his Master's Service, *having a Scar in his Face*, and is suspected to have taken away several Sums of Money. Whoever secures him, and gives notice to his master Mr. Thomas King of Chalgrave in Oxfordshire, within 7 miles of Oxon, or to Mr. William Saunders at the Peacock in Clare-Market, London, shall have two Guineas Reward, and Charges.

(London Gazette, 16/20 Oct. 1690)

The condition of these disfigured or scarred black slaves suggests the reason why they ran away.

In modern times, the tradition of violence has continued, in the race riots of 1919, the 1950s and the 1980s. 'England is the last colony of the British Empire' as E.P. Thompson put it; the patterns of mutual antagonism and violence which characterized the periods of colonization and imperialism are still at play in Britain today. Some British newspapers respond to this violence by blaming the blacks, who have been overwhelmingly the victims of racism and white inhumanity. Hence the *Daily Telegraph* of 7 April 1980, reflecting on the Brixton and Bristol riots commented:

These unfortunate West Indian migrants emerged in the aftermath of slavery without any stable family framework to integrate into a wider society. Lacking parental care many ran wild. Incited by race relations witch-finders and left-wing teachers and social workers to blame British society for their own shortcomings, lacking the work ethic and perseverance, lost in society itself demoralised by socialism, they all too easily sink into a criminal sub-culture.

The violence against blacks takes many forms. At its crudest and most frequent levels are the daily physical attacks on individuals, communities and property. The burning of homes with their occupants, occurs with alarming frequency. The fire at a Deptford home in January 1981, in which thirteen young black people perished, has come to symbolise such violence, but also to symbolise the apathy of the majority white population to the death of fellow citizens and human beings. Scarcely a week passes in Britain nowadays without news of the burning down of one Asian household.

Violence also takes the form of the exertion of pressure which affects the mind and can lead to mental disintegration. Keeping black people distant from the mainstream of national life, by ill-funded educational provisions, slum housing, denial of capital to black businesses and denial of employment, creates enormous resentment in the black community, and acute mental distress. It is no wonder that black people are 'over-represented' in the mental hospitals and psychiatric wards of British prisons, in a similar proportion to their 'under-representation ' in areas of education and employment.

Major Texts

1. Linton Kwesi Johnson 'Rage' in *Dread Beat and Blood* (London: Bogle L'Ouverture Publications, 1975)

A history of white oppression of the African is engraved enduringly in the memory of the present-day black man in England. Feelings of rage accumulate, the psyche is deeply troubled, existing at the edge of dangerous explosion:

> Soon some white one will stroll by,
> and strike he will to smash
> the prison wall of his passion
> and let his stifled rage run free

The reference to the 'white one' indicates the impersonality with which black and white people react to each other. The black personality, under the pressure of racism has been reduced to the impersonality of a clenched fist:

> he waits with rage
> clenched tightly in a fist.

2. Faustin Charles 'Cricket's in my Blood' in *Days and Nights in the Magic Forest*. (London: Bogle L'Ouverture Publications, 1986)

Faustin Charles, born in Trinidad, has spent most of his life in London, but his poems are still set overwhelmingly in the West Indies. All the same, many of them are obliquely about a British experience. Charles uses the West Indies as a metaphor for the expression of passions invoked and nurtured in Britain. 'Cricket's in my Blood' (with 'Viv') for example, is more about the violence of New World history than about the game of cricket. The opening and closing lines convey the mood of the violence of the game and of its appreciation by the West Indian:

Blood Fire!
. . . . . .
The volcano erupts
And blows the game apart.

The energy of violence is beautifully captured in the verse, recreated in the rhythm of its lines: 'Bat on beat, clash, ball bouncing century'; 'Hooked by the torrent of slashes'; 'the game swells with blood'. The first passage in the poem explicitly locates such violence of cricketing within wider 'black' experiences of victimization to conquest and sacrifice:

Rising to conquer, propelled by a gift
And a hunger,
The ball swerves, lifts, and strikes
Widens with pain and anguish
Breaking heights beyond the sun,
And the light circles all,
Screaming in the extremity
Of lives laid out bare in the height of sacrifice.

There is allusion here to Imperialist conquest, fuelled by 'gift' of possession and the 'gift' of a 'superior' civilization, a 'superior' science which enables that possession by conquest; allusion too to pre-Columbian Aztec and Mayan rituals, and by implication the interruption of these savage rituals by the new savagery of the Conquistadors. These ideas of New World violence are further pressed home in a series of images suggesting rapine and swordfight: 'The batsmen's plunder' 'The play tightens my soul into steel'. The poem, together with 'Viv' (on Viv Richards, the legendary batsman) and 'Greenidge' (on Gordon Greenidge, another genius of the bat), is among the finest ever written by a

Caribbean poet, achieving a rare imaginative penetration into the layers of New World history. Charles, by writing and publishing the poem in England, is indicating that historic patterns of violence are still in play in England today.

3. Creswell Durrant 'Colours' in *News for Babylon,* ed. James Berry (London: Chatto and Windus, 1984)

A short poem on the Notting Hill riots, exploring the impersonality of violence. 'Them' refers to the rioters, the 'metropolitan' to the police. In this inhumane landscape the poet is a witness to his own humanity: 'I saw it', he writes, the 'I' being the personal, the individual as opposed to the impersonal 'eye', and 'it' being the dead weight of impersonal violence. Lines like 'nothing could stop them until the blood flowed' brilliantly evoke a descent into inhumanity. The poem ends superbly with the observation of the early morning after the riots, when two council workmen pause from their task of cleaning up to drink some shared milk:

> two crossing sweepers black and white
> filling their brotherhood at a milk machine.

4. Desmond Johnson 'Mass Jobe' in *Deadly Ending Season,* (London: Akira Press, 1984)

An old man looks back at a wasted life in England where he had first arrived with hopes of self-betterment. The West Indian immigrant experience is described through the variety of back-breaking work they endured: train-shunting, office cleaning, road sweeping, can-packaging, house building. Although they ran the transport system, they themselves did not move on, did not progress or arrive at the destination of prosperity:

> we were railman
> railwoman
> train drivers
> Signal man
> and controller
> collector of tickets
> and night workers

        our best years spent
        on british rail
        our years went by
        . . . .
        we have nothing to show
        not a penny.

The old man contrasts the patient endurance of his generation
with the violent activity of the new generation in the Bristol and
Brixton riots, and finds optimism in the resurgence of the spirit
of rebellion:

        I know they shall win
        and overcome,
        but for us it's late
        to say 'if we know'
        much too late to make a show
        just thank massa God
        that mi live so long
        to have a walk with the wife
        still feeling strong
        holding the wife
        by a bus stop stand
        going to friends
        in the heart of Brixton
        Railton Road
        our new Kingston.

3. Martin Glynn 'Madness Tek Over' in *De Ratchet A Talk*,
   (London: Akira Press, 1985)

Glynn, a young poet working in the 'dub' mode, writes simply of
a black underworld of crime, prostitution, violent confrontation
with the police, inner-city decay, hustling and drug-peddling.
He laments the loss of pride, strength, achievement in the
community which crumbles under the stress of poverty and
racism. When the final pressure comes, when the community is
finally put against the wall, it will have no resources to overcome
extermination by the whites (the Holocaust experience is hinted
at in the poem):

De weak gwane fall
de weak gwane bawl
only strong survive
but de strong get weak
de future look bleak
NOW MADNESS START ARRIVE

E. Homage to Ancestors

To one exiled to a new land and existing under severe duress, the dream of returning home, to a condition of freedom and kinship with natural community, is obsessive. Many slaves committed suicide, believing that by their deaths they would be reborn and reunited in Africa with their families. When the East Indians were shipped over to work in the sugar plantations of the West Indies, many too longed for their period of indentureship to end, so that they could return home. The colonial statistics of mortality indicated that many Indians died of 'homesickness'.

Many West Indian writers of the 1950s and 1960s felt the deep urge to return 'home', (Africa and India) to explore ancestral roots and heritage. Some like Edward Brathwaite and George Lamming actually undertook the voyage, and their sojourns in Africa nourished their writings. They were able to draw upon and utilize the resources of ancestral traditions, ancestral myths and religious symbolism in reclaiming wholeness of identity, wholeness of personality. For others, like Naipaul the return to India was deeply disturbing and disappointing.For Naipaul, the wounded civilization of India, with its dirt and decay, only reinforced his West Indian sense of loneliness.

Black Britons have also been pulled to their countries of origin. In the eighteenth century, the resettlement of blacks in Sierra Leone in 1787 represents one (sordid) aspect of the 'return journey'. The community of black poor, centred in St. Giles, London, was offered a tempting scheme, backed by promises of money, to return to Africa. It was in reality an attempt to purge London of its black population by voluntary repatriation: some four hundred blacks, frustrated by their poverty, fired by the emotion of returning 'home', and urged along by the payment of small sums of money, joined the ship. The expedition however, from the beginning, was ill-equipped, and there had been allegations about the misappropriation of funds by the white managers of the project. As James Walvin explains:

> The transportation and equipping of the expedition gave scope for further exploitation of hapless, innocent people. When they arrived the settlers found the land inhospitable and their freedom at risk from slave traders. Those lucky enough to survive the ravages of the first year were abandoned by their white leaders. News of the appalling experiences of the settlers soon reached the black community in London - indeed their sufferings actually began on board ship in the Thames. Cugoano complained bitterly about their treatment and noted that news of the undertaking was unlikely to encourage further emigration from London.

> Organisers of the Sierra Leone settlement had employed Equiano as a respectable link-man with the black community but his battle against the corruptions of the undertaking swiftly led to his dismissal.

The nineteenth century saw the beginnings of the Pan-African Movement in Britain when black leaders from America, the West Indies and Britain, sometimes with the crucial support of Asians, organized a series of Congresses in London, then in Europe, the outcome of which were calls for the end of Imperialism and the withdrawal of Europeans from Africa. The Movement was a reflection upon the psychological need of people of the African diaspora to recreate links with their homeland. In its later stages Pan-Africanism, outwardly a political movement, took on the philosophical tenets of 'negritude', which argued for the existence of a recognizable 'Africanness' of black people ('Africanness' in terms of, for example, a shared subconscious memory).

In modern times, the British-born generations of blacks have been unsettled by Immigration and Nationality laws which seem designed to question their status as citizens, question their rights of abode, and indeed, rights to their civil rights. In addition, the pressure of racism, and rejection by the white majority, have encouraged many black people to assert pride in an African or West Indian heritage, as both an act of self-discovery and of defiant self-discovery. Instead of locating their spiritual lives in Britain, they do so in the West Indies or Africa. The growth of a Rastafarian culture in Britain is a testimony to this process of spiritual relocation. Many throw off their 'slave-names' and 'white clothing' and adopt African names and modes of dress. Some deliberately reject the scientific-materialist and technological civilization, which they perceive as the heartless, commercial creation of the white man, and live an 'alternative' existence of a 'communion with nature'. Britain becomes Babylon, the whore, the slaver, the land of cleavage, spiritual sodomy and sadomasochism, from which blacks must liberate themselves by the rediscovery of holy, and whole, ancestral values.

Major Texts

1. Armet Francis 'Mister Blacman' in *The Black Triangle: The People of the African Diaspora,* (London: Seed Publications, 1985)

Francis is a photographer by profession, and *The Black Triangle* is a stunning collection of photographic images of Africa, Jamaica, the United Kingdom and the United States of America. Francis writes in the Preface to his book, 'As a black person living in Britain from the age of eight, I learnt to be conscious of myself in a very negative way.' His photographs strive to convey the humanity of the African individual. 'The feelings conveyed', he writes, 'are of the common human condition. Trying to show the quiet inner suffering of You and I, the simple human feelings. That is the basis of my work.'

In 'Mister Blacman', one of the poems accompanying the photographs, Francis looks back to the experience of slavery, the claustrophobia of the slaveship, the cheapening of human life and the breaking of community. It is this ancestral experience, and his kinship with the experience, which is the source of his art and expression. Out of the tragedy of ancient suffering comes the creativity of the new generation.

2. Morgan Dalphinis 'Re-Exiled: Nigeria' in *For those who will come after,* (London: Karia Press, 1985)

Dalphinis, born in the West Indies, has lived a great part of his life in Britain. His subsequent return to Africa is a journey of great expectation and profound sorrow. Nigerian corruption leads to despair, he is disgusted by the materialist squalor of the people and the degeneration of idealism:

Mercedes is king,
The whorehouses are full,
The rumshop, self-suicide
Replaced by the beerclubs,
And the fat opulence of
Suicidal consumers.

He was once a speck of dust exiled from Africa in the heap of enslavement. Now, his return to Africa, instead of being a humane moment, a moment of rebirth, is sordid and impersonal:

Back again,
A dust returns to dust.
Returns to flies
And a black prostitute.

Whore who kills her
Children living.
Murderess,
Killing even the
Foetus of her creation.

'Mother Africa', the symbol of the yearning of the exiled Afro-West Indian, is in reality a whore - consumer of Western toys.

3. David Dabydeen *Slave Song* (Denmark and UK: Dangaroo Press, 1984; Reprinted 1986).

A collection of poems in creole which looks back to an Indian childhood in Guyana, and to the central experience of canecutting (the Indians arrived in the Caribbean from 1838, upon the emancipation of slaves, to work in British-owned sugar plantations). The canecutter becomes an ancestral symbol of exploitation and endurance, thus the inheritor of West Indian traditions, Amerindian and African. The brokenness of the creole recreates the broken desires of the canecutter: 'his life is a constant flow of desire and a constant frustration of desire. He will remain dreaming in the mud and awakening to the mud'. The poems are accompanied by an introduction, translations and detailed critical notes, the poet's strategy being to possess wholly not just the imaginative recovery of ancestral experience (the poetry) but the intellectual 'explanation' of that experience (the translations and literary criticism). The latter, which seeks to exclude the literary critic and historian by taking on their function, has political significance: it seeks to expose by implication the long tradition of English literary criticism and historiography which falsifies or misrepresents (through ignorance or biases of judgement) black experience; it seeks too to banish the 'middlemen' from the 'business' of poetry ('middlemen' being, in other guises of merchant or trader, the creators of slavery and indentureship in the Caribbean).

4. Fred D'Aguiar *Mama Dot* (London: Chatto and Windus, 1985)

Poems from another poet of Guyanese origin which look back to childhood experiences in Guyana. Mama Dot is a mother-figure, the terror but also the wisdom and protector of the children; her folk-knowledge preserves life:

> I am knotted in pain
> She measures string
> From navel to each nipple
>
> She kneads into my belly
> Driving the devil
> Out of my enforced fast.

Although some of the poems verge on sentimentalism or romantic nostalgia (hence the weak Wordsworthian echoes in 'Guyanese Days' - 'my shaded spot' - or the hollow imitation of Keats in the same poem - 'Now I shake a Downs-tree bending ripe / My head bent as its marble-sized fruits'), others reveal a keen sense of the naivety and sheer irresponsibility of childhood.

5. James Berry 'Confession' in *Chain of Days,* (London: Oxford University Press, 1985)

Chain of Days is 'about the colonized, the colonizer, and the person that emerges'. The book draws on the experiences of both new and old worlds. From Africa, slavery, colonization, and life

163

in America and Britain, the poet gathers and reassesses a past and present and reclaims a self.' In 'Confession', a black child, brought up in the racist environment of England is able, by accident, to move away from her sense of 'otherness' towards a sense of her kinship with humanity. The racism of England has led her to believe that black people are incompetent, useless, cursed:

> ... I was born to know
> black people had nothing. Black people
> couldn't run their own countries,
> couldn't take part in running the world.
> Black people couldn't even run
> a good two-people relationship.
> They couldn't feed themselves, couldn't
> make money, couldn't pass exams
> and couldn't keep the law.

One day she sees by chance a painting in a book depicting West Indian people in a state of poverty and struggle, and with this discovery comes the realization of experiences shared between blacks in Britain and the West Indies. She is not 'peculiar', nor is the condition of her race in Britain unique. In the struggle of the West Indian people she finds the purpose of her own life.

F. The New Language

The use of language as an index of the levels of civilization of its speakers dates back to ancient times. The term 'barbarian' is derived from a Greek word meaning 'to speak like a foreigner'. Anyone who did not speak Greek was a barbarian. In even earlier days survival itself could hinge on the ability to pronounce a word properly: in the *Book of Judges*, Ch. 12, v. 4, when the Ephraimites are slain in their thousands by the Gileadites, the inability to pronounce a syllable identified those who were to be protected from those who were to be slaughtered.

> And the Gileadites took the fords of the Jordan against the Ephraimites. And when any of the fugitives of Ephraim said, 'Let me go over', the men of Gilead said to him, 'Are you an Ephraimite?' When he said 'no' they said to him, 'Then say Shibboleth', and he said Sibboleth', for he could not pronounce it right; then they seized him and slew him at the fords of the Jordan. And there fell at that time forty-two thousand of the Ephraimites.

The term 'shibboleth' subsequently passed into common usage and now means a test word or opinion or principle, the use of or inability to use, revealing one's party or nationality or orthodoxy. Words, in other words, include or banish people from protective society, words can validate or exterminate them.

In more recent times it is black people who have been subjected both to exclusion from the definition of civilization, and to genocide, on the basis of language. Early English travel books on Africa described the primitive habits of the natives and the absence of language simultaneously. In 1634, Sir Thomas Herbert suggested that Africans and apes mated with each other, the evidence for this being that African speech sounded 'more like that of Apes than Men ... Their language is rather apishly than articulately founded.'

In the eighteenth century, which was the Age of Slavery as well as the Age of the Dictionary, such attitudes to Africans were sustained, the link between barbarism and lack of speech made explicit. *Spectator* No. 389 of May 1712 described Hottentots as 'Barbarians, who are in every respect scarce one degree above Brutes, having no language among them but a confused Gabble, which is neither well understood by themselves or others.' Many passages in the anthropological literature of the period focus on descriptions of the monstrosity of their organs of speech as well as their organs of propagation. Whilst John Ogilby is writing about the 'large Propagators' sported by the men of Guinea and Richard Jobson on male Mandingoes being 'furnished with such members as are after a sort burdensome unto them', William Strachey focuses on their 'great big lips and wide mouths'. Thick lips and monstrously misshapen mouths, sometimes, as in the case of the anthropophagi, located in their chests, indicated their inability to make proper speech. Interestingly, when we find eloquent and civilized blacks in English literature of the period, as in the case of Mrs. Aphra Behn's Oroonoko, their physical features are more European than African:

> His mouth, the finest shaped that could be seen;
> far from those great turn'd lips which are so
> natural to the rest of the Negroes

We also recall that Othello, Oroonoko's predecessor, was also enmeshed in concepts about language and civilization. At the point where he felt most removed from Venetian society, he breaks down and cries out, 'Haply for I am black / And have not those soft parts of conversation / that chamberers have'. In the eighteenth century, the 'soft parts of conversation' were the most valuable index of civilization. The Group Portrait or so-called Conversation Piece was the latest form of painting, populated by gentlemen and ladies engaged in card-playing, tea-drinking and polite conversation.

In eighteenth century poetry, 'wit' was the most valued component; as Alexander Pope puts it, 'true wit' is 'what oft was thought but ne'er so well expressed.' And Samuel Johnson's *Dictionary* was a landmark in locating the word at the centre of civilization. Given this centrality of the word, the apparent wordlessness of the Africans was deemed to be incontrovertible evidence of their barbarism.

The equation between African and animal, sustained by the issue of language, which gave moral validity to the Slave Trade, continued in the nineteenth century, the Age of Imperialism and Anthropometrics. Africans' skulls, lips, teeth and mouths were scrupulously measured by leading white scientists to reveal their cultural and moral primitivism and therefore the necessity of continuing colonial rule. Science underpinned the Imperial process. However it was also quite obvious that Africans had language, and this posed a problem to white conceptualization since language *was* an undeniable *human* characteristic. Professor Bernth Lindfors illustrates the problem by reference to the case of the San people of South Africa, a group of whom were brought to Britain between 1846-50 to be displayed at circuses and fairgrounds. The speech of the San visitors was their most noticeable feature: 70% of it consisted of a set of implosive consonants, commonly called 'clicks', which were absent from the English phonological system. Lindfors, quoting an authority on the subject, states that 'The number and variety of these click consonants, complicated still further by subtle vowel colorings and significant variations in tone make it, from the phonetic point of view, among the world's most complex languages'. To the Victorians however, hardly interested in such analysis, San speech merely sounded like animal noises. The *Liverpool Chronicle* (5/12/1846) reported that 'The language resembles more the cluck of turkeys than the speech of human beings', and *The Era* (6/6/1847) described the language as 'wholly incomprehensible, for nobody can interpret it ... The words are made up of coughs and clucks, such as a man uses to his nag. Anything more uncivilized can scarcely be conceived.' Even when admission of their humanity was grudgingly conceded, the classics of white literature were raised against the San people: *The Observer* of 21st June 1847 wrote that 'their distinguishing characteristic as men is their use of language, but besides that, they have little in common ... with that race of beings which boasts of a Newton and a Napoleon, a Milton, and a Dante.'

Milton and Dante are sufficient to put blacks in their place. But even when, as in the eighteenth century, black writers revealed an ability to write in the style of the white classics, their literature was still scornfully dismissed. Francis Williams, for instance, a black man educated at Cambridge in the first half of the eighteenth century, largely through the curiosity of his patron, the Duke of Montagu, who wanted to find out 'whether, by proper cultivation, and a regular course of tuition at school and the university, a Negro might not be found as capable of literature as a white person'. Francis studied classics at an English grammar school then mathematics at Cambridge University, where he also became famous for his composition of Latin odes, a practice which he continued on his return to Jamaica. Francis Williams' classical attainments were however disputed by David Hume who declared that 'In Jamaica indeed they talk of one negro as a man of parts and learning; but it's likely he is admired for very slender accomplishments, like a parrot, who speaks a few words plainly.' Literature written by blacks in European classical vein could therefore only be hollow mimicry.

David Hume's dismissal did not however affect twentieth century West Indian writers who continued in the tradition of Francis Williams's classicism. Whilst European writers, artists and musicians were turning away from classical symbolism, which had become dead and meaningless, and turning to Africa, India or China for inspiration, the emerging West Indian writers were busily discovering classical mythology. Ezra Pound, mourning the impossibility of classical civilization in modern Europe explores instead Chinese philosophy; T.S. Eliot ransacks Frazer's *The Golden Bough* for pre-classical fertility images or else explores Sanskrit sources; D.H. Lawrence leaves England in search of pre-Columbian Indians; Picasso and others are startled into originality and *modernism* by the shapes of *ancient* African sculpture; meanwhile West Indian writers were wading through the rubbish-heap of books that the Europeans had discarded from their libraries, and finding Homer and Horace. In Frank Collymore's 'Hymn to the Sea', the Caribbean sea is heard and viewed through a classical sensibility - its high surf recollects the horses of the Titans and Aphrodite is born from its foam. The West Indies has been the dumping ground of white mythologies (El Dorado, Prospero, Crusoe) and our early writers would seem to have revelled in the rubbish. Their purpose in fact was a profound one: to reveal the 'classicism' (and all that 'classicism' betokens in terms of virtue and quality) of West Indian life at a time when the West Indian was deemed to be an inferior species of humanity. Their purpose too was to assert that European philosophy and concepts could find root in the West Indies; that the West Indian peoples were (and had been from the beginning) open to receiving the best of Western civilization. Finally, these writers were using Western classical forms to show their similarities with pre-Columbian and African myths, thus breaking down the historically destructive boundaries based on race, colour and nationality. This latter motive was, at one level, deeply humane; at another level, the writers were attempting to reveal the life of the imagination, at the level of creation of symbol and myth, being a human capacity, irrespective of racial or national origins. Arawak myth *was* Western Classical myth, different in appearance but identical in substance and capacity.

There was also, however, in those early days, a movement away from the apparent 'colonial' influences which produced such 'classical' poetry.In March 1931, a Trinidadian magazine under the editorship of Albert Gomes, *The Beacon*, attempted to instigate a movement for 'local' literature. *The Beacon*, in the two years it ran, was most influential: each edition sold between 1,500 and 5,000 copies. It constantly encouraged literature that was 'authentic' to the West Indian landscape, and to the daily speech of its inhabitants. 'We fail utterly to understand', an editorial of January/February 1932 commenting, on the quality of short stories received for publication, 'why anyone should want to see Trinidad as a miniature Paradiso, where grave-diggers speak like English M.P.'s.' Emphasis was placed on the use of creole, and on a realistic description of West Indian life, for political and aesthetic reasons. To write in creole was to validate the experience of black people against the contempt and dehumanizing dismissal of white people. Celebration of blackness necessitated celebration of black language, for how could a black writer be true to his blackness using the language of his/her colonial master? The aesthetic argument was bound up with this political argument, and involved an appreciation of the energy, vitality and expressiveness of creole, an argument that Edward Brathwaite has rehearsed in his recent book, *The History of the Voice* (New Beacon Books, 1984). For Brathwaite the challenge to West Indian poets was how to shatter the frame of the iambic pentameter, which had prevailed in English poetry from the time of Chaucer onwards. The form of the pentameter is not appropriate to a West Indian environment: 'The hurricane does not roar in pentameters. And that's the problem: how do you get a rhythm which approximates the natural experience, the environmental experience?' The use of creole, or Nation language, as he terms it, involves recognition of the vitality of the oral tradition surviving from Africa, the earthiness of proverbial folk speech, the energy and power of gestures which accompany oral delivery, and the insistence of the drumbeat to which the living voice responds.

All this would seem to limit Caribbean poetry to an implosion or explosion of sound without significance, an anarchy that banishes the logic, order and intellectuality of *contemplative* verse. Caliban, as it were, becomes content with his stereotype of being a loud-mouthed and performing savage, devoid of the intricacies of intellect. John Figueroa has ridiculed Brathwaite's position in his poem 'Problem of a Writer Who Does Not Quite', exposing the dangers of limiting the range of Caribbean poetry, or legitimizing only one form of expression, which he sees as a form of self-inflicted racism. Figueroa's plea is for the retention of the European classics - Homer and Horace - as literary models. Naipaul sympathises with this position. He adamantly refuses to limit himself to local colour, local imagery and local language, and pours scorn on one West Indian writer whose 'women swayed like coconut trees, their mouths the colour of sapodilla, the inside of their mouths the colour of cut star-apple, their teeth white as coconut kernels, and when they made love, they groaned like bamboos in high wind.' Naipaul's point is that the creative imagination is capable of ranging beyond the boundaries of actual experience, and that its encounter with otherness is a vital expanse and adventure. The business of the writer is to break through the confines of narrowness, whether it be the political narrowness of nationalism, or the cultural narrowness of localism, or the imaginative narrowness of social reality, or even the existential narrowness of reality itself.

Other writers from the West Indies or South America lend direct or oblique support to Naipaul's view. Borges for instance adamantly refuses both to be Argentinian and to be naturalistic. 'We cannot limit ourselves to purely Argentine subjects in order to be Argentine', he declares, refusing to populate his stories with gauchos and descriptions of pampas. Borges's alternative is 'a surrender to that voluntary dream which is artistic creation', a dream which can range through cultures and societies or transcend them totally, a dream which can take shapes and forms unrelated to political, social or cultural issues, contemporary or ancient, a dream which can be physical or metaphysical. C.L.R. James adds his distinctive voice to the debate, claiming that the West Indian consciousness is a component of European sensibilities which created it. The West Indies is the creation of

Europe, and therefore European philosophy, aesthetic forms and languages are as native to the West Indies as to Europe. It is as natural to teach *The Tempest* in Bermuda, as it is to teach it in a Somerset classroom. The West Indian heritage is a plural one, and the language of West Indian literature can take whatever form it pleases, depending on the purposes of the writer. Creole, in other words, is no more natural or local or native than Queen's English. James' description of some of his Trinidadian contemporaries who were fluent in classical tongues, in some instances more so than the Europeans, is borne out by Eric Williams in an autobiographical anecdote relating to his undergraduate days at Oxford, when all the undergraduates in his class were given a Latin test - translating a few lines from Ovid - in preparation for their Latin examination. After the test, Williams is summoned to the tutor's room, and a white fellow-student, obviously prejudiced in his belief that the English language was hard enough for a Trinidadian, never mind Latin, offers Williams patronizing sympathy:

Student:	What happened, poor chap?
I:	He told me not to return to the class.
Student:	Dear, dear, are you that bad?
I:	No, I am that good.
Student:	I don't understand.
I:	He says that I can pass the examination standing on my head and so he wants me to take it [earlier than normal] at the end of term.
Student:	I don't believe it.
I:	You see, we speak Latin in Trinidad.

Eric Williams's anecdote, as Shiva Naipaul says, betrays his colonial mentality; Williams's dignity in declaring 'You see, we speak Latin in Trinidad', is 'the dignity of the colonial; and more particularly, of the black, slave-descended colonial. It is an ambiguous attitude: an extricable mixture of envy, yearning and sullen resentment; the feelings, in a word, of an orphan'. Nevertheless, the point is that Latin *is* native to Trinidad, Latin is part of its West Indian and European heritage. The slave-owners made sure of that when they called their black slaves Caesar, Pompey or Horace. The irony is that the West Indian has taken the debased experience of being immersed in Latin for reasons of parody, and turned it inside out, becoming learned and distinguished in the language, and finding literary and inspirational meaning in the classics.

Black writers in Britain are confronted with the same issues as that facing the West Indian writers in the 30s onwards. Living in a society which alienates and threatens them, black people have developed their own mode of speech which they can use to communicate with each other but which they can equally use to exclude white listeners. There is a parallel here with the use of language by slave communities in the West Indies: the slaves evolved a language close enough to English to prevent punishment by their white masters (speaking in African tongues was banned on the plantations) but distant enough from English to allow them to communicate secretly with each other, to plot and conspire against their masters. Black British language is also an assertion of strength in ancestry, an assertion of self-sufficiency and spiritual independence. The writers are aware that the creole of the West Indies was not broken and inferior English; quite the opposite: that creole, whilst using English diction retained many of the grammatical structures of African and Asian languages. The use of creole in their writing therefore is one way of linking up with their West Indian, and ultimately, their African or Indian past and heritage. They consciously spurn 'standard English', not because they are incapable of utilizing its resources, but because of the passionate urge for independence in a society that would reduce them to a new servility; a society that has become accustomed to rubbishing or neglecting any aspect of historic black endeavour.

Major Texts

1. John Agard 'Listen Mr. Oxford don' in *Mangoes and Bullets*, (London: Pluto Press, 1985)

A hilarious defence of creole against the prejudices of academic English, which, below the surface humour deals with the pernicious stereotypes of black criminality. 'Me not no Oxford don' Agard declares in creole defiance, 'Me a simple immigrant / from Clapham Common'. He didn't 'graduate' he 'immigrate': in this play on words Agard is deliberately echoing the charge that black speech is full of malapropisms and badly-learnt English. He assumes the role of a (literary) mugger, petty criminal and person prone to violent behaviour, a role and image common in the popular white imagination:

I ent have no gun
I ent have no knife
but mugging de Queen's English
is the story of my life
....

Dem accuse me of assault
on de Oxford dictionary /
imagine a concise peaceful man like me ?
dem want me serve time
for inciting rhyme to riot

Agard's poetry is deeply rooted in oral forms of expression: he calls himself a 'Poetsonian', drawing attention to the relationship between his poetry and the calypso. In the Preface to *Mangoes* he writes of a

kinship with the satirical spirit & folky surrealism of the calypsonian ... The whole resurgence of the oral art in poetry has caused black poets to come up with words of their own making. You can think of jazzoetry / Gil Scott-Heron calls himself bluesician or bluesologist / you also got dub poetry, using reggae beat /rapso poetry / & a number of white poets call themselves ranters. Not that anything is wrong with the word poet. Is just that most people have come to see 'poet' & 'poetry reading' in very distant cerebral terms. So using these other terms I just mentioned is like subverting the expectations of audiences. Is a way of reclaiming other art forms into poetry like theatre & not treating poetry as isolated. So Ntozake Shange, for instance, describes her work as choreopoem or poemplay / incorporating dance & drama / and I describe a long children's poem I did recently, growing out of different musical instruments, as a poemsemble.It's nothing new really, it's a return to ancient traditions, a return to the troubadour & the shaman / shawoman.

173

2. Benjamin Zephaniah *The Dread Affair* (London: Arena, 1985)

A collection from a leading exponent of 'dub' poetry which uses nursery-rhyme rhythms, reggae-beats, African drum-sounds and other resources of orality, such as the rhythm of Old Testament psalms (see the poem 'Dread eyesight' for the music of the Bible). Zephaniah is also attentive to the strange music of the body's organs (see the poem 'Sounds keep sounding.')

3. Brother Resistance *Rapso Explosion* (London: Karia Press, 1986)

Trinidadian born Brother Resistance is equally inspired by the relationship between words and music. Rapso is 'network of rhythms where the rhythms of the voice blend with African drums and the rhythms of the Steel Drum/Pan. This base is called *Foundation Rapso* and it has taken to a more intense musical form with the blending-in of stringed instruments'. Brother Resistance reads / performs in Britain to enthusiastic applause, but has also been criticized for 'masking the superficiality of his ideas and badly crafted poetry by a fraudulent alliance with music'. Poetry,it is argued, has its own inner sound and should not depend on external props like the drums:

> It is not
> It is not
> It is not a good poem

as Derek Walcott recently put it, in ridiculing the kind of poetry that is accompanied by drumming. In any case, it is argued, no amount of association with music or evocation of 'folk' traditions can disguise clichéd expression and tedious rhetoric. These criticisms, which include accusations about the writing of doggerel, have also been levelled against Zephaniah's poetry, and to a lesser extent, Agard's.

4. Valerie Bloom *Touch mi: Tell mi* (London: Bogle L'Ouverture, 1983)

A collection of poems in creole, some sensitively crafted, on a variety of social themes. Bloom adopts the role of social commentator and gives witty, humorous or scathing views on life in the Caribbean and Britain. She does not force music into or upon the poem, depending instead on the natural warmth and energy of the speaking voice; hers is the balladry of Robert Burns, Claude McKay and Louise Bennett.

5. Rudolph Kizerman 'A story from the Tribe' in *News for Babylon* ed. James Berry, (London: Chatto and Windus, 1984).

The poem tells the story of the masks worn by a black man. To begin with he is a Westernized intellectual, with an abstract and elitist vocabulary, a 'borrowed rhetoric / refined pauses / and his obsequious exposition / of eloquent irrelevance / in the Great Tradition':

> From the wealth of his received
> philosophical vocab',
> he'd only find time to expatiate
> on semantics,
> dialectics,
> somebody's empiricism.

Times have changed however, in the climate of the radical 60s, and the black man adopts the gestures of radicalism:

> lost his neck-tie
> and gained a word;
> he frequently says fuck, nowadays,
> and wears a dashiki.

His language is now 'roots' in the extreme; he has moved from one rhetoric to another:

> now, he turned on
> to familiar black scenes;
> he switches on
> such hip jive
> you'd hardly believe:
> cool it
> swing it,
> groove it,
> dig it,
> screw it,
> knock it,

        rip off,
        pig,
        motherfucker
        right on.

Kizerman's poem explores language as the ground of identity,
and his concern is with the schizophrenia of the black man living
in white society: the initial aspirations of belonging to a white
culture (which is deeply racist), then a desperate attempt to
recover 'African' modes of being.

Select Bibliography

A. West Indian Literature

Edward Baugh: *West Indian Poetry 1900-1970* (Savacou, 1977)

Lloyd Brown: *West Indian Poetry* (Heinemann, 1984)

David Dabydeen (ed.): *A Handbook for Teaching Caribbean Literature* (Heinemann, 1987)

Michael Gilkes: *Wilson Harris and the Caribbean Novel* (Longmans, 1975)

Michael Gilkes: *The West Indian Novel* (Twayne Publishers, 1981)

Louis James (ed.): *The Islands in Between: Essays in West Indian Literature* (Oxford University Press, 1968)

Hena Maes Jelinek: *The Naked Design: A Reading of 'Palace of the Peacock'* (Dangaroo Press, 1976)

Bruce King (ed.): *West Indian Literature* (Macmillan, 1979)

Kenneth Ramchand: *An Introduction to the Study of West Indian Literature* (Nelson, 1976)

Kenneth Ramchand: *The West Indian Novel and its Background* (Faber, 1970)

Anna Rutherford and Kirsten Holst Petersen (ed.): *Enigma of Values: The Work of Wilson Harris* (Dangaroo Press, 1975)

Ivan Van Sertima: *Caribbean Writers* (New Beacon Books, 1968)

John Thieme: *The Web of Tradition: Uses of Allusion in V.S. Naipaul's Fiction* (Hansib, 1988)

Landeg White: *V.S. Naipaul: A Critical Introduction* (Macmillan, 1975)

B. Black British Literature

E. Cashmore and B. Troyna (ed.): *Black Youth in Crisis* (London, 1982)

David Dabydeen: *Hogarth's Blacks: Images of Blacks in Eighteenth Century Art* (Dangaroo Press, 1985, reprinted Manchester University Press, 1987)

David Dabydeen (ed.): *The Black Presence in English Literature* (Manchester University Press, 1985)

Peter Fryer: *Staying Power: The History of Blacks in Britain* (Pluto, 1984)

Prabhu Guptara: *Black British Literature: An Annotated Bibliography* (Dangaroo Press, 1986)

F. Shyllon: *Black Slaves in Britain* (Oxford University Press, 1974)

J. Walvin: *Black and White: The Negro and English Society 1555-1945* (Allen Lane, 1973)

Index of Authors

INDIA IN THE CARIBBEAN
edited by Dr David Dabydeen
and Dr Brinsley Samaroo

A joint publication by Hansib and the University of Warwick Centre for Caribbean Studies this collection of essays, poems and prose by leading Indo-Caribbean scholars and writers, on East Indian history and culture in the Caribbean, was published to commemorate the 150th Anniversary of the arrival of Indians in the region (1838-1988). Indians have made significant contributions to the politics, culture and economic progress of the region, some of which are documented in this important publication.

326 pages 13 illustrations (black and white)
ISBN 1 870518 00 4 PB   £8.95
ISBN 1 870518 05 5 HB   £11.95

COOLIE ODYSSEY
by David Dabydeen

Dabydeen's first book of poems, *Slave Song* was awarded the Commonwealth Poetry Prize and Cambridge University Quiller-Couch Prize. *Coolie Odyssey,* his second collection, probes the experience of diaspora, the journeying from India to the Caribbean then to Britain, dwelling on the dream of romance, the impotence of racial encounter and the metamorphosis of language.

52 pages
ISBN 1 870518 01 2 PB   £3.95

THE WEB OF TRADITION:
USES OF ALLUSION IN V.S. NAIPAUL'S FICTION
by Dr John Thieme

A new and exciting study of one of the Caribbean's major and most controversial novelists, V.S. Naipaul, who has won several of the world's literary prizes including the Booker Prize.

Thieme re-explores major novels like *In a Free State* and *A House for Mr Biswas* locating them within Western literary traditions and at the same time revealing their essential Indian-ness.

224 pages
ISBN 1 870518 30 6 PB   £6.95
(Published jointly with the Dangaroo Press.)

THE SECOND SHIPWRECK: A STUDY OF INDO-CARIBBEAN LITERATURE
by Dr Jeremy Poynting

A wholly original and pioneering study of Indo-Caribbean literature dealing not only with the works of well-known writers like Sam Selvon and the Naipaul brothers (in fiction) or the two Dabydeens (in poetry) but with a host of lesser known but equally talented writers, including women writers who are studied here for the first time.

approx 280 pages
ISBN 1 870518 15 2 PB   £6.95

THE OPEN PRISON
by Angus Richmond

Angela, a sensitive and disturbed child, growing up on the estate of her white guardian in British Guiana, is slowly and painfully awakened to a society in turmoil, in which both black and white are struggling to reassert their roles during the period of economic instability prior to the First World War. As a mulatto, the child of a loveless union between black and white, the situation is even more problematic. Only after a desperate early marriage generates a series of tragic events, does Angela learn to understand the ultimate possibilities of her own displaced identity.

This novel received a GLC Award in 1985 when it was still in typescript form.

232 pages
ISBN 1 870518 25 X PB   £4.95

FROM WHERE I STAND
by Roy Sawh

A moving autobiography from one of Britain's leading black spokesmen and a notable orator at Speaker's Corner, Hyde Park. Sawh details his upbringing in the plantation environment of Guyana and his subsequent migration to Britain where he experiences rejection and imprisonment for his outspoken attacks on the injustice of racism. Sawh's book adds to a growing list of black autobiographies which have their origins in the slave narratives of the eighteenth century. It is unique in being the first Indo-Caribbean autobiography published in Britain, a literary milestone.

94 pages 24 illustrations (black and white)
ISBN 0 9956664 9 1 PB   £5.95

THE IDEOLOGY OF RACISM
by Samuel Kennedy Yeboah

A comprehensive and well-researched study of the history of peoples from the American diaspora, listing outstanding achievements in the fields of arts, science and technology. It traces the origin and development of Western racism, the ideology which underpins it, and the power which makes it operable. This book is a major contribution to Multicultural Educational Studies and of great interest and will appeal to the general reader.

approx 292 pages
ISBN 1870518 07 1 PB   £8.95
ISBN 1870518 08 X HB   £11.95

THE GREAT MARCUS GARVEY
by Elizabeth Mackie

Marcus Garvey was one of the great black leaders of the twentieth century, a powerful influence on the development of black pride and black power in America and the Caribbean, and on Pan-Africanism in general. Maligned, harassed and hounded throughout his life, Garvey died in loneliness and poverty. He did not live to see the independence of Africa and the Caribbean, a cause he gave his life for.

120 pages 10 illustrations
ISBN 870518 50 0 PB   £4.95
A Hansib Educational Book

SPEECHES BY ERROL BARROW
edited by Yussuff Haniff

A collection of speeches made by the late Barbadian Prime Minister, Errol Barrow, over the past three decades in which his involvement in Caribbean politics and his vision for the future are noticeably highlighted. Through his speeches we see Errol Barrow as a true Caribbean man, fighting for the region's independent identity.

200 pages
20 illustrations (black and white)
ISBN 1 870518 70 5 HB   £10.95

INSEPARABLE HUMANITY
AN ANTHOLOGY OF REFLECTIONS BY
SHRIDATH S. RAMPHAL
edited by Ron Sanders

Inseparable Humanity is an anthology of reflections by one of today's leading thinkers, Shridath Ramphal the Commonwealth Secretary-General.

Few contemporary figures have written and spoken on so many themes of critical importance to the maintenance of world order and for the prospects of human survival on a basis of equity and social justice.

approx 400 pages
ISBN 1 870518 14 4 HB   £14.95

THIRD WORLD IMPACT 8th Edition
edited by Arif Ali

Third World Impact has long established itself as the only fully comprehensive work of reference regarding the presence of the visible minorities in all spheres of British life.

For the eighth edition a number of exciting new features are being planned to make it a qualitative advance on previous issues with the work ranging over questions of the police, legal rights, education, immigration and nationality legislation, prisons, housing, trade unions, the arts and culture, women and sports. An invaluable reference section includes the biographies of well over 1,000 prominent members of the minority communities, a guide to more than 100 Third World countries and the names and addresses of thousands of community organisations, of London Embassies and High Commissions, etc.

Third World Impact will be of equal value to the general reader and the diligent researcher. Historians of the future will certainly see it as the black community's answer to the 'Doomsday Book'.

approx 500 pages fully illustrated
ISBN 1 870518 047 HB   £15.95